I0558242

The Peaceable Kingdom?
A History of Terrorism in Canada from Confederation to Present

Phil Gurski

DOUBLE‡DAGGER
— www.doubledagger.ca —

To all the men and women in CSIS, the RCMP and other law enforcement agencies in Canada who have worked in counterterrorism and helped to keep the true north strong and free.

Library and Archives Canada Cataloguing in Publication
Gurski, Phil author
The Peaceable Kingdom? / Phil Gurski

Issued in print and electronic formats.
ISBN: 978-1-990644-48-1 (hardcover)
ISBN: 978-1-990644-46-7 (soft cover)
ISBN: 978-1-990644-47-4 (e-book)

Editor: Patricia Walsh / Phil Halton
Cover design: Pablo Javier Herrera
Interior Design: Winston A. Prescott

Double Dagger Books Ltd
Toronto, Ontario, Canada

www.doubledagger.ca

Table of Contents

Preface..i
Foreword by Ward Elcock, former Director of CSIS.................................iii
Introduction..1

1 | The Canadian Counterterrorism Landscape.......................................14
2 | Ethno-Nationalist Terrorism..32
3 | Islamist Terrorism..72
4 | Other Forms of Terrorism...138
5 | Counterterrorism Challenges..152
6 | Final Thoughts..171

Acknowledgements..175
Appendix - Listed Terrorist Entities in Canada.....................................176
Notes..180

Preface

NOT MUCH HAS CHANGED on the terrorism landscape since the first appearance of this book: there have been some minor additions, primarily in the chapter on other forms of terrorism (Chapter 4) and counterterrorism challenges (Chapter 5).

It may strike some as odd that a publisher with an emphasis on military books has agreed to (re)issue a book on terrorism. After all, is terrorism, at least in the West, not largely a concern for security intelligence and law enforcement agencies (i.e. spies and cops)?

No.

As I wrote in 2019 in An End to the War on Terrorism, the military forces of many countries play a significant role in counter terrorism, mainly abroad but also at home. Furthermore, as the frequent targets of terrorist groups, usually Islamist extremist ones, our women and men in uniform are often at the forefront of (counter)terrorism.

I hope this addition to the growing Double Dagger collection is as valued as its other titles. As a former Canadian terrorism analyst, I feel it is important to tell Canadian stories. Double Dagger is doing just that and I commend them for it.

Phil Gurski
Russell, ON, October 2022

Foreword

IN 1989 I BECAME RESPONSIBLE FOR SECURITY and intelligence issues in the Privy Council Office, as what was then known as the Coordinator for Security and Intelligence. Now, more sensibly, the position is known as the National Security Advisor. Five years later in 1994, I became the Director of the Canadian Security Intelligence Service (CSIS). At a stroke, I left the practice of law to spend the next twenty-two years in a number of national security-related positions which proved to be both challenging and rewarding.

In 1989, counter-intelligence issues were still the priority in Canada. Indeed, to make the point, my appointment followed on, at least in part, from a pyrrhic counter-intelligence victory in which Canada had expelled some seventeen Russian intelligence officers. Predictably, the Russians responded by expelling an equal number of Canadians which decimated the Department of External Affairs' Russia program, as diplomats who had not yet even been posted to Moscow were declared persona non grata. In the result, the position of Coordinator became vacant.

Terrorism was, however, even then more of an issue than most Canadians understood. While our first brush with terrorism dated back almost to Confederation, as Mr. Gurski notes, most Canadians were unaware of it. While the October Crisis of the 1960s was a more recent memory, it was also only a memory in the late 1980s, even if some of the consequences still reverberated. Even the bombing of Air India Flight 182 in 1985 and attacks by Armenian terrorists on Turkish diplomats and facilities in Canada, while appalling to most Canadians, were not seen as attacks on Canada. When the prime minister of the day wrote a letter of condolence to the prime minister of India, it ignored the reality that most of the passengers on Air India were Canadians, the attackers were

Canadians and the terrorist organisation, the Babbar Khalsa, was founded in Canada.

Beyond those two groups which carried out violent attacks in Canada, the truth was that an 'alphabet soup' of terrorist organisations operated, or had sought to operate, in Canada over the years. Because they targeted immigrant communities and eschewed violence in Canada they were, however, beyond the consciousness of most Canadians outside those communities. The closest most Canadians came to a terrorist organisation was likely the collection of donations for 'widows and orphans' in an Irish pub, given that those donations were more likely headed to the Irish Republican Army (IRA).

Nevertheless, those organisations did affect Canada and Canadians, even if they avoided violent attacks. Often, they abused Canadians in immigrant communities, like the Tamil Tigers who were well known for extorting funds from the community for the campaign of violence in Sri Lanka (linked to a desire for an independent Tamil homeland). In other cases, intelligence organisations from the former homelands of many immigrant communities sought to target those communities fearing that some in those communities might contribute to terrorist campaigns in their former homelands. Terrorism and its consequences were therefore a growing focus for the Service, even if most Canadians were unaware of that reality.

In the mid-to-late 1990s a host of new individuals and organisations became a more serious concern. Islamist dissidents from Algeria but also other North African states who had been forced to leave their homelands were in turn pushed out of the European countries from which they had sought to continue their opposition to North African regimes. Some who had also trained or fought in Afghanistan, Bosnia or Chechnya began to find their way into Canada, particularly Montreal, as many were French speaking. Their backgrounds quickly made them a major counterterrorism concern. How serious was to become clear in early 1999, when Ahmed Ressam, an Algerian trained by Al Qaeda (AQ) in Afghanistan, was arrested crossing into the United States to bomb Los Angeles airport.

That arrest brought AQ to the attention of Canadians and made it clear that there was, unlike most other terrorist groups that had operated in Canada, a new group which wanted to target the United States. The events of September 11, 2001 (9/11) were to make that reality even clearer and reminded us, as Canadians, that, as well as protecting all Canadians from terrorism, it was also important for us to ensure that our southern border was not used as a route to attack the United States.

Notwithstanding all that followed from 9/11, the reality for Canadians, even as AQ and later the Islamic State of Syria and Iraq (ISIS) declared Canada a target, was that Canada had never suffered a major attack. Apart from the occasional reminder of the risk of such an attack, Canadians again began to see terrorism as something that happened elsewhere—in Paris, London, New York, or Moscow but not in Canada. Unfortunately, they are likely wrong. While there is no obvious easy explanation as to why we have never suffered a major attack, one hopes that in part it was a result of the efforts made to prevent such an attack. Realistically, however, it is likely that it was the simple abundance of soft targets in other more important countries that saved Canadian cities from a major attack.

While both AQ and ISIS have been pushed into the fringes of the world, they have not been defeated and in some areas, such as the Sahel, they are becoming stronger and attacks, while not as major as those in the past, are still being reported. There is, therefore, a continuing risk of an attack in Canada. While every effort will I am sure be made to prevent such an attack, it is true, as an IRA member once observed, that terrorists need only to succeed in one out of ten attempts to be successful, while security services need to prevent all ten to be successful. Since that is a high bar, the likelihood of achieving it is correspondingly low, so neither the absence of a major attack to date nor the efforts of security services are guarantees that there will not be an attack in the future.

Given that I believe that terrorism still poses a serious risk to Canada and its interests, I believe that it is important that Canadians be better informed about the threat from terrorism. Mr. Gurski, whom I know as a very capable and experienced analyst on the subject, is uniquely well-placed to contribute to that goal. Having served in both the Communications Security Establishment (CSE) and CSIS, Mr. Gurski brings to the discussion his experience of actual investigations which, while some of what transpired must remain secret, will, inevitably, better inform the discussion of terrorism and impact on Canada and Canadians.

Ward Elcock
Director of CSIS, 1994 to 2004

Introduction

TERRORISM. THAT ONE WORD has become part of our daily vocabulary over the past few decades in ways that would have seemed unthinkable to most of us at another, earlier time. The cataclysmic events of September 11, 2001 (9/11) in New York and Washington, when violent extremists wounded the very soul of the United States (US) and killed thousands in the process, are why we today hear and read a lot about terrorism. One cannot peruse any mainstream news source on any given day and not come across at least one item that is related to a terrorist attack somewhere in the world.

As already noted, this was not always the case. Prior to 9/11, terrorism was very much a niche phenomenon, something that happened "over there." While terrorist acts certainly predated the Al Qaeda (AQ) attacks on American soil by at least a century and a half (when the term "terrorism" began to enter common parlance), for most of us it did not seem part of our reality.

Sure, there was the odd incident here and there and most countries did witness an attack every now and then (some more than others), but the world of terrorism was simply not something most of us worried, or even cared, about. It was just not important enough to dedicate significant resources to, or to take up so much of our news feeds. As far as we were concerned it was not that important as it was not unfolding in our backyards (or front yards for that matter).

What a different world we live in now!

As noted, if one looks at any news source—dailies, journals, websites, etc.—one will be hard-pressed to find a day where there is not a story (or more likely several stories) on terrorism. Trust me, I spend a few hours every day doing so, and I cannot remember the last time I did not share information about a terrorist incident (usually on Twitter but also in blogs and podcasts) - or more hopefully, counterterrorism successes— and usually several such incidents on the same day.

It has been said that 9/11 changed everything, and that is certainly true when it comes to our exposure to the world of ideologically motivated violent extremism. We now obsess about terrorism, often in counterproductive ways, and our governments have enacted new laws, new policies and new overseas military engagements, all aimed at "defeating" terrorism.

Included in this response has been use of the unfortunate term war on terrorism. I do not intend to rehash the arguments on why this coinage has been less than helpful: my fourth book An End to the War on Terrorism provides in depth analysis. Suffice to repeat that our collective tendencies to declare war on common nouns (drugs, poverty, coronavirus, etc.) rarely end well, if at all.

Some Places Do Suffer from a Lot of Terrorism

Nevertheless, it is indisputable that a few of the world's 200-odd nation states do witness a disproportionate number of terrorist movements and terrorist attacks. The list of those states will scarcely come as a surprise to the reader: Afghanistan, Syria, Iraq, Somalia, and Nigeria, as well as increasingly that area of Africa known as the Sahel (Niger, Mali, Central African Republic, Burkina Faso), are usually at or near the top of annual summaries of terrorism worldwide (a good reference is the Institute for Economics and Peace's *Global Terrorism Index*).[1]

The reasons why these countries, and not others, are afflicted with higher levels of terrorism are complex and beyond the scope of this book. Still, poor governance, discrimination and inequality, outside interference (in the form of a foreign military presence, and those who support terrorists logistically or financially), and historical grievances all play a part.

After you get past the top dozen or so states, the terrorism incidence scale tends to drop off. Many, many nations see little or no terrorism at all. Japan is a good example, with the spectacular exception of the Aum Shinrikyo chemical attacks in the 1990s and a few others. Japanese counterterrorism officials rarely contributed anything to the conversation at G7 meetings of the counter-terrorism group in the 2000s which I attended—and this was not solely due to language difficulties in English.

In other countries the level of terrorism will vary from year to year as acts of ideologically or religio-politically motivated violence stemming from different groups or individuals ebb and flow. Some nations are home to multiple movements often in direct competition or rivalry with each other (far-right terrorism and Islamist terrorism for example, which both seem to be vying for top spot in our attention spans in many Western countries as of 2023).

If we limit our discussion to the West, broadly defined, we see differences as well. The United Kingdom (UK), for instance, once faced a significant threat (now largely muted, albeit not entirely absent) from Irish nationalist terrorism. It then experienced a spate of Islamist terrorism, still very much a challenge, which may now be followed by right-wing violent extremism, growing in part in the post-Brexit environment and the misguided notion of a "pure" Britishness (anti-immigrant and especially anti-Muslim).

Most other Western nations have similar violent extremist landscapes, largely dominated in recent years by Islamist terrorism with a much smaller (for the most part, although that may be shifting) far-right milieu: some scholars and pundits are convinced the latter will soon usurp the former (I am not one of them, however, and I am confident I have the data to support my position).

In none of these countries is the threat of terrorism to be considered existential in nature, unlike, perhaps, Afghanistan where the Taliban which has re-emerged as the government of that nation. Let us recall that the Taliban is very much a terrorist group, implying that it would be one of the rare cases of such an organisation in control of a nation state.

As an aside, the Islamic State of Iraq and Syria (ISIS)—known variously as the Islamic State of Iraq and the Levant (ISIL), and simply "Islamic State" (IS)—once thought it was a nation in its self-styled caliphate (or "califake" as one of my contacts likes to call it). Still, this was not the same as a terrorist group governing a recognised nation.

"Not an existential threat" does not imply "unimportant." Western nations all have an array of security intelligence and law enforcement agencies (sometimes the two are folded into the same organisation as we will see) mandated to investigate terrorist threats and prevent attacks from taking place. Each country has its record of successfully foiled plots and court prosecutions followed by the incarceration of terrorists. Each country, alas, also has a litany of attacks that went undetected in the planning stage, leading to the deaths of innocent civilians.

Which Brings Us to Canada

I would imagine that Canada evokes many images for most readers—big, natural beauty, politeness, and "not America"—but that "terrorism central" is not one of them. In truth, there have been very few acts of terrorism in Canada in which people died or were injured over its entire 150-plus years of existence. When that is compared to the other Western nations with which it is usually associated, this country comes out looking pretty good.

And yet Canada has not been immune from terrorism. Acts have taken place within its borders and Canadians have participated in terrorist actions abroad. Interestingly, the ideologies underlying these acts run the gamut from Islamist extremism to the far right, environmental extremism, and nationalist terrorism.

Why this broad range of terrorist movements? To those familiar with the Canadian mosaic (often contrasted with the US melting pot) this should come as no surprise. As Mr. Elcock noted in his foreword, Canada has become home for many seeking a new life (or fleeing persecution) from the proverbial four corners of the world, and a small number of those have brought homeland conflicts and hatreds with them. On rare occasions, such grievances have been translated into attacks here, some of which led to the deaths and injuries of Canadians. Other attacks were planned and perpetrated by what some call "homegrown" terrorists—i.e., those born and raised in Canada. Still others were carried out by Canadians, some with ties to native lands, who went back to those countries of birth to sow death and injury.

This book will look at the history of terrorism in Canada since its independence in 1867, i.e. what we call Confederation. It will focus on acts, planned, foiled or successful, in this country, as well as those carried out by Canadians in other lands. As the emphasis is on actual attacks, there will be no discussion of other aspects of terrorism such as logistic or financial support, both of which are interesting and present in Canada, but which are beyond the intended scope. Mr. Elcock noted in the foreword that many terrorist groups ranging from the IRA to the Liberation Tigers of Tamil Eelam (LTTE) were active in Canada over the years, have been the subject of investigation by the security services, but have not carried out any action of a terrorist nature in this country. Hence, these will not feature here. This is not to imply that terrorist financing is not an important issue which should be investigated and punished (Canada, to my knowledge, has a very poor record in this regard).

The time span to be examined is a century and a half—that is, the entirety of the history of Canada as an independent nation. As we shall see, Canada's first act of terrorism occurred before it celebrated its first birthday. The discussion will continue to the present day and will endeavour to be as up-to-date as possible by the time of publication.

My Contribution to the Discussion

One of the strengths I believe I bring to this topic is my experience working in security intelligence in Canada for more than thirty years. I was a multilingual foreign intelligence analyst with this country's signals intelligence (SIGINT) agency, Communications Security Establishment (CSE), from 1983 to 2001, where I developed a capability in both Arabic and Farsi (Persian) and a specialisation in the Muslim world, although I did not work in counterterrorism while at CSE (more on this later). Following that part of my career, I worked as a senior strategic analyst at the Canadian Security Intelligence Service (CSIS) from 2001 to 2015, specialising in Islamist terrorism and homegrown violent radicalisation. The bulk of this book will feature CSIS and its counterterrorism efforts, many of which I had a front-row seat to observe (and contribute somewhat to, if I may be so bold to say). I also had short stints at the National Security Directorate within Public Safety Canada, working on counterterrorism policy and in community outreach, and as a terrorism advisor with the Provincial Anti-Terrorism Section (PATS) of the Ontario Provincial Police (OPP).

Given my background, this will not be an academic look at terrorism in Canada, but rather will provide a practitioner's perspective. Unlike a typical academic work there will be no literature review or discussion on methodology in this book. As a result, with the sole exception of a small section of Chapter 2 there will be no reference to academic work at all on the phenomenon of terrorism in this country. The reasons for that one exception will become obvious to the reader at the time. In all other instances I have elected to include the thoughts, reflections, and experiences of actual counterterrorism practitioners, including my own, in these discussions.

Based in large part on my experiences and exposure to counterterrorism at CSIS, I have to date written five books on terrorism:

- The Threat from Within: Recognizing Al Qaeda-inspired terrorism and radicalization in the West (Maryland, USA: Rowman and Littlefield, 2016)

- Western Foreign Fighters: The Threat to International and Homeland Security (Maryland, USA: Rowman and Littlefield, 2017)
- The Lesser Jihads: Bringing the Islamist extremist threat to the world (Maryland, USA: Rowman and Littlefield, 2017)
- An End to the War on Terrorism (Maryland, USA: Rowman and Littlefield, 2018)
- When Religion Kills: How extremists justify violence through faith (Colorado: Lynne Rienner, 2020)

The approach I have used to date is to look at publicly available information on terrorism and to subject that data to the filter and scrutiny of a former intelligence analyst. I have never sought to put terrorist acts or terrorist groups and individuals through a theoretical framework and will not do so here either.

Furthermore, with the exception of the terrorist act examined at the very beginning of Chapter 2, all the incidents occurred during my lifetime (I was born in December 1960) and, hence, I have had some exposure to or experience with them. Even more narrowly, with the added exception of parts of 2, these events took place while I was working in security intelligence for organisations mandated to investigate threats of this nature. This afforded me a somewhat rare insight into these deeds not afforded to the average Canadian.

In addition to my own viewpoint, I had my own "sources," referred to as "contacts" in this book to avoid confusion with sources involved in investigations. Many of the people I spoke with were former colleagues of mine at CSIS, some of whom I worked alongside in counterterrorism, although I also had exchanges with members of the Royal Canadian Mounted Police (RCMP) and a few others who worked in other Canadian government departments (there is even some input from a few foreign counterterrorism officials). Their experiences, as well as my own, imply that the discussion of terrorism in Canada will by definition be CSIS-centric. As there are other agencies in this country which play a role in the detection and neutralisation of terrorism plots (see next chapter) there are other voices yet to be heard. I believe this focus to be a natural one in this context as well as the one with which I am most familiar and hence most qualified to weigh in on. I have always tried to limit my comments to areas I consider I know well and on which I have something intelligent to say. Consequently, I will not stray into areas where this is not the case. If others with similar operational experience eventually decide to weigh in, that will also constitute a much-needed perspective on this aspect of Canadian history.

It is also important for the reader to understand the context of what my role was, especially at CSIS. Throughout my career I was an analyst, starting as a tactical hands-on one and ending more as a strategic specialist. My job was to take raw intelligence and, at least at CSE, translate it into English, summarise the most important information, and provide it to clients. Later, at CSIS, I looked at all the intelligence in our database on a daily basis as it related to terrorism and considered what it all meant. I would regularly write strategic pieces that informed clients about the big picture of what we were seeing.

I was not an investigator (i.e., intelligence officer or "IO"). The IOs were responsible for recruiting and running human sources and carrying out investigations. My role was to capture what they learned in ways that made sense to those who read our intelligence product. Nevertheless, it is vital to point out that I developed very close working relations with many IOs across Canada, chatting with them daily on their efforts and seeking clarification. In fact, I would often hear from my colleagues that they appreciated my input to their efforts ("I am so glad someone is reading my reports!"). As my knowledge and specialisation increased, I was asked more and more to participate in human source debriefings, a task I welcomed.

In addition, thanks to my ease with and enjoyment of public speaking I was regularly asked to represent CSIS locally, nationally, and internationally, at conferences and meetings on terrorism. I believe that, to date, I have delivered thousands of briefings and presentations on Islamist terrorism around the world, as well as participated in thousands of interviews with Canadian and foreign media outlets.

My contacts, for the most part, were former IOs. These men and women were at the forefront of investigations aimed at keeping Canada safe. Their knowledge is without equal in this country and their stories need to be told. I humbly endeavour to do so here.

At the same time, I must refrain from providing too much detail on some of the comments I make in this book. Much of my understanding of terrorism came from classified material which I am not authorised to disclose. This included access to human source information, intercepted communications, and other secret intelligence. It should not come across as puzzling why I am unable to delve into these details: secret is secret after all. I will, however, talk about what I read and what I wrote in ways that do not contravene the Official Secrets Act.

As an aside, I recently read a review for a book on the Indian intelligence agency known as RAW (Research and Analysis Wing) in which the individual charged with weighing in on the value of this contribution to intelligence studies wrote: "This book is recommended for readers interested in Indian intelligence but is somewhat frustrating for scholars. . . . The sourcing and methodology are problematic and make the book challenging to review. . . . The use of unattributed interviews and codenames makes it all but impossible to confirm the veracity of the stories."[2]

There is little question that some may react in a similar way to this book. However, I believe the reader will see the usefulness of viewing this phenomenon of terrorism in Canada through the perspective of people who have worked in counterterrorism in the country.

This is, then, a relatively short book on terrorism in Canada over the last century and a half. It really should be much longer, thousands of pages longer. That it is not, is driven by two primary factors: that so much of the material on terrorism cases in Canada remains classified, and that no one wants to read a book that is several thousands of pages long.

In summary then, all the incidents discussed here refer solely to the following activities:

- terrorist attacks carried out in Canada;
- planned (and foiled) terrorist attacks in Canada that are part of the public record;
- terrorist attacks planned, and/or carried out abroad in which a Canadian was involved and which are part of the public record; and
- Canadians who elected to join terrorist groups abroad and who are part of the public record.

The reasons for this narrow scope should be obvious to the informed reader.

As an analyst at CSIS I was privy to hundreds of thousands of pieces of information that were tied to that organisation's counterterrorism mandate as well as intelligence shared with us by Canadian and international partners. While the bulk of this information—everything not freely available—must remain secret, I will draw, carefully, on what I know about these non-public cases to illustrate a point.

At times sections of this book will come across as "anecdotal." The word is anathema to many academics, and in a 2019 podcast with the head of the University of Maryland's START Consortium, a former CIA employee, Gary LaFree, and current academic Marc Sageman dismissed the use of anecdotes as unimportant[3]. I could not disagree with Mr. Sageman more, and in all honesty, as a former CIA employee he should have known better when he said this. Here it is a strength. I have clear memories of what I was thinking and doing, along with my operational colleagues, when investigations in Canada were unfolding. In my many discussions with former colleagues they too "told stories." I believe that sharing some of these experiences will enhance, and not detract from the book. The reader will naturally decide if it does.

This is not the first book on terrorism in Canada. Several others come to mind and should be noted. Canadian journalist Stewart Bell has written two such accounts: *Cold Terror*[4] and *The Martyr's Oath*[5]. Mr. Bell continues to be Canada's premier terrorism reporter and much of the open-source material included here to provide backdrop to my comments was taken from his published work (both in the *National Post* and later for Global News). There are also several previous offerings on the Front de libération du Québec (FLQ) in Quebec and the Air India attack (see Chapter 2). To the best of my knowledge this is the only comprehensive history of terrorism in Canada dating back to the country's creation and continuing to the present, as seen through the experiences of a former intelligence analyst and others who worked in national security.

How is Terrorism Viewed in Canada?

I have already stated that over its 150-year history Canada has been relatively immune from terrorism. While clearly more has gone on behind the public's scrutiny, meaning that terrorism is actually bigger than what makes it to the nation's newspapers, it is nonetheless a small problem. Consequently, getting the citizenry to take notice has not always been the easiest of jobs.

People care when things go wrong. An excellent example of this transpired as my research for the book was taking shape: the April 2020 mass shootings in Nova Scotia, one of Canada's eastern Atlantic provinces. The deaths of twenty-two innocent people at the hands of a gunman gave rise to speculation and accusations that the RCMP, the police force of jurisdiction in Nova Scotia, made mistakes that led to unnecessary deaths. In law enforcement and security intelligence, after all, you are only as good as your last (perceived) failure. When you get it right and stop an act of terrorism from transpiring, you receive little credit (and often the opposite as some will raise accusations of overreaching or heavy-handedness). Get it wrong, however, and everyone is screaming for your head.

A few deaths have occurred on Canadian soil as a result of acts of terrorism, but even those did lead to questions as to why the perpetrators were not stopped. These will be discussed in the appropriate chapters. There has also been criticism over cases that were successful in nature but perceived by some as overkill: these too shall be examined.

There has also been widespread criticism of the RCMP and CSIS over alleged "mistakes" in which Canadians suffered mistreatment abroad and in which these agencies played a role: several inquiries have been held which have raked these agencies over the coals (the Arar Inquiry, the Iacobucci Inquiry, etc.). These commissions found that intelligence was improperly shared with foreign powers, which allegedly led to the imprisonment and torture of Canadian citizens.

While I do not agree with many of the inquiries' findings, all these cases have been well discussed in the public record, and hence will not be covered here. The jury of public opinion has cast its verdict and there is nothing more to say. I will weigh in, however, on the so-called "national security certificates" to some degree in the penultimate chapter.

In addition, and perhaps somewhat surprisingly to some, at various times in Canadian history the government of the day was not always seized with the reality of terrorism. I can speak to this from direct personal experience. Those of us working in counterterrorism endeavoured to impress upon decision makers in the early 2000s what our investigations had taught us about how and why some Canadians were embracing violent Islamist extremist views and at times our analysis was dismissed.

Part of the complacency was tied to the somewhat immature intelligence culture in the greater Canadian government (outside the security services themselves). Canada simply does not have the same regard for and use of intelligence that many of its allies do. There were also those who rejected just about anything coming out of CSIS: some would balk at not being allowed to learn more about sources and methods while others preferred CIA or MI6 (British Secret Intelligence Service) material to anything Canadian organisations could produce.

Maybe things are better now: I am, after all, almost six years into my post-intelligence retirement. I certainly hope so. I will return to this issue of public perception and weak intelligence culture in Canada in the penultimate chapter.

Structure of the Book

Where possible, the chapters of this book will flow chronologically. The ability to organise terrorism in Canada in this way is facilitated by the fact that the different kinds of violent extremism outlined here follow one after the other, more or less. Deviations from this plan will be minimal and, I hope, self-explanatory.

The first chapter outlines how terrorism is handled in Canadian law and provides a brief history and description of the agencies tasked with investigating and preventing it. In Chapter 2, I discuss what I am calling "nationalist" or "ethnic" terrorism, ranging from the very first attack in Canada less than a year after its birth, to Quebec independence, Sikh extremism, Armenian terrorism, and others. In Chapter 3, by far the longest chapter, I tackle the complicated Islamist terrorist presence in Canada, as well as those among my fellow citizens who left to join terrorist groups abroad, some of whom carried out terrorist acts. Chapter 4 will examine far-right and far-left terrorism as well as other lesser-known brands. The challenges in counterterrorism operations will be presented in Chapter 5. At the end of this book is a short conclusion on where Canada has been, where it is now, and a tenuous speculation on where it might be headed when it comes to terrorism.

Just a note about spelling: I have elected to use British-Canadian spelling throughout the book, including, for consistency, in quotations.

A Note on Sourcing

As already stated, much of the material in this book originated either from my own direct experiences with intelligence-led counterterrorism investigations or through the experiences of men and women with whom I worked at CSIS and other security intelligence and law enforcement organisations. I am willing to reflect on, and disclose, more information than is usually associated with those who work in security intelligence, an industrymore often typified by statements such as "no comment" or, the more tongue in cheek, "I'd tell you but then I'd have to kill you." Hence, my thoughts and reactions constitute a significant portion of this book.

Also, as noted, there is a lot that came from the experiences of my colleagues. I spoke with many at length, and the history of counterterrorism in Canada presented here is richer because of their contribution. I agreed to keep these contacts anonymous: this explains the lack of footnotes. These individuals, who have worked in counterterrorism in CSIS or the RCMP, either at the HQ or regional level, or abroad during the time periods covered, were all very generous with their time and very open with their comments. One thing rang true: they all were very proud of what they did to help keep Canada and Canadians safe.

In addition, I have tried to include open sources to provide background on individual cases. In each instance I once had access to far more secret material than that which made it into the news cycle but cannot disclose the sources. It suffices to say that if I have cited a particular open-source news item it is not inconsistent with what we collectively already knew thanks to investigations and investigative techniques (human sources, warranted intercepts, etc.). Nevertheless, a handful of Canadian journalists who focus on national security and terrorism are to be congratulated for their tenacious reporting: Canadians are better informed as a consequence.

One More Thing . . .

When people ask me about my career in intelligence in Canada, I have a consistent answer: I had a job where for 32 years I could not wait to get to work every morning. I was exposed to very highly classified information. I was asked to weigh in on very important matters. I worked alongside some truly outstanding Canadians. My tasks varied tremendously over more than three decades—I was, in order of task, a multilingual analyst, a cryptanalyst, the head of SIGINT collection, a strategic terrorism analyst, and an outreach advisor. I got to see all of Canada and the world and have in-depth conversations with my Canadian and international counterparts. I was accorded many amazing opportunities. In short, I was a very lucky Canadian.

This should not be misconstrued to suggest that everything was perfect. It was not. I had some down times as well, reporting to some less-than-stellar supervisors: not everyone I met at CSIS was a great person. In this respect, I am confident that CSIS is no different than any other work environment around the world. As they say, a few bad apples do not necessarily spoil the whole bunch.

In addition, I am not so naïve as to think that CSIS as an organisation is perfect either. Mistakes were made. In the end, however, I remain convinced that the men and women who work there do their utmost to help keep Canadians safe. No one that I knew ever deliberately tried to engage in activity that was not consistent with the CSIS mandate or that was contrary to Canadian law. Any mistakes identified by later courts or inquiries were, in my opinion, errors of omission, not commission. Not everyone agrees with this assessment.

Hence, I will not engage in much criticism of Canada's counterterrorism community in this book. That may disappoint some who were looking for a "kiss and tell" account intended to shock and appall Canadians. This is not that book.

In December 2020 as I reviewed my contact interviews and relistened to the recorded interviews and reread my notes, I realised that there was much I could have included that I have elected not to. My interlocutors told me so many stories about so many individuals and so many investigations that I found myself rewriting parts of the book. At the end of the day, I had to make choices and some readers may take me to task for not writing about case X or terrorist Y. While I have tried to be as comprehensive as possible, I make no pretensions that this book is exhaustive.

Now to turn to the crux of the matter. Canada has sometimes been referred to as the "peaceable kingdom." Let us now look to those times when it was not.

1

The Canadian Counterterrorism Landscape

The Security Service which has been part of the RCMP will be removed and established as an independent non-policing agency whose mandate is to gather intelligence bearing on threats to the security of Canada. A specialised organisation is required to respond to the increasingly sophisticated nature of threats to our security.
- Robert Kaplan, former Canadian Solicitor General

IN THIS CHAPTER WE WILL LOOK AT which agencies are responsible for the lion's share of terrorism investigations in Canada and how they interact. Terrorism may not have constituted a large part of security intelligence and law enforcement resources historically, but neither was it entirely ignored.

Who "Does" Counterterrorism in Canada?

In a book that purports to look at the history of terrorism in Canada, it is important to understand which agencies have the lead in carrying out investigations that aim to identify and stop terrorist actors before they strike. As this book will examine terrorism from a practitioner angle, a skeletal overview will help to explain who does what to prevent terrorists from succeeding.

Each country has its own mechanisms in place and Canada is no different. In addition, given that we will be looking at the phenomenon of violent extremism over a 150-year span, it is inevitable that these mechanisms will have changed: recall that the phenomenon of terrorism as most specialists define it really began to develop in the latter half of the 19th century. This time period happens to coincide with the emergence of Canada on the international stage as an independent nation. Suffice to say that for the purposes of the general reader the main agencies in Canada today are CSIS, the RCMP and CSE.

It is important to note that for much of our history, terrorism was simply not a major concern for the Canadian government nor even for its security and law enforcement agencies. The reasons for this are very simple: with minor exceptions, terrorism has not been that prevalent in Canada until very recently. Even when it was becoming so in other parts of the world (e.g., Ireland in the 1970s and 1980s, Afghanistan in the 1990s, etc.), it did not resonate that strongly here. This is not to say that it was entirely absent, as the substantive chapters of this book will demonstrate, but the need to protect Canada from terrorists and terrorist attacks was a pale shadow of a much greater priority for security agencies: counter-espionage and counter-intelligence (CI) were long the number one tasks, especially during the Cold War. This theme will be developed much more in the chapters to come.

Terrorism in Canadian Law

Given that terrorism appears to be a ubiquitous phenomenon these days, it might be assumed that we have always had to deal with it. As already noted, this is not true: most scholars (such as US academic, David Rapoport) date its onset to the mid-19th century. Despite this century and a half of terrorist activity, laws to punish terrorism, whether the acts are foiled or successful, are also fairly recent additions to criminal codes.

In Canada there was no specific terrorism offence in the Canadian Criminal Code in the pre-9/11 period. As we shall see, terrorism in this country predates the attacks in the US in 2001, but there were other legal mechanisms to deal with it.

The first inclusion of terrorist activity in the Criminal Code does not appear until after the events in New York and Washington. For some in Canada, the enormity of those events and the alacrity with which the law was passed resulted in a far from perfect piece of legislation (more on this later). It should also be emphasised that terrorist activity and not terrorism is defined. The relevant sections of Canadian law start in Section 83.1. The following extracts are the most important for the purposes of this book:

> *83.01 (1) terrorist activity means . . . (b) an act or omission, in or outside Canada, (i) that is committed (A) in whole or in part for a political, religious or ideological purpose, objective or cause, and . . . (ii) that intentionally*
>   *A. causes death or serious bodily harm to a person by the use of violence,*
>   *B. endangers a person's life,*
>   *C. causes a serious risk to the health or safety of the public or any segment of the public,*

D. causes substantial property damage, whether to public or private property, if causing such damage is likely to result in the conduct or harm referred to in any of clauses (A) to (C), or
E. causes serious interference with or serious disruption of an essential service, facility or system, whether public or private, other than as a result of advocacy, protest, dissent or stoppage of work that is not intended to result in the conduct or harm referred to in any of clauses.

There are subsequent sections on terrorism financing and "participating, facilitating, instructing and harbouring" terrorists or terrorism. Having terrorist offences in the Criminal Code has not always made terrorism prosecutions easy; in fact, it is often quite the opposite.

I will not weigh in on the nature of legal tools to combat terrorism in Canada. But, to my mind, security intelligence and law enforcement agencies were engaged in counterterrorism work for decades before a law prohibiting it was drafted. These organisations did so in keeping with their mandates, which in turn were based on pieces of legislation. Besides, as terrorism usually involves a serious act of violence there have always been ways to deal with it in the absence of a formal legal definition of terrorism. Murder (or conspiracy to commit murder) is a crime on its own, and those intent on killing can be investigated, arrested, charged, and prosecuted on that ground alone. Interestingly, the crime of subversion was also used to investigate what is clearly terrorism.

A Brief History of Counterterrorism Agencies in Canada

On July 1, 1867, Canada consisted of four provinces: Ontario, Quebec, Nova Scotia, and New Brunswick. Manitoba and the Northwest Territories joined in 1870 (Nunavut split off from the Northwest Territories in 1999), followed by British Columbia in 1871, Prince Edward Island in 1873, Yukon in 1898, Alberta and Saskatchewan in 1905, and Newfoundland in 1949.

Public safety was the domain of a combination of provincial and municipal forces, some of which predated Confederation. The North West Mounted Police (NWMP) saw the light of day in 1873 and was tasked with keeping the peace in Western Canada. The NWMP eventually became the RCMP: the two organisations have been with us for almost the entirety of

Canada's history as a nation.

According to RCMP historian S. W. Horrall in the summer 1985 edition of the RCMP Quarterly, just prior to the emergence of the NWMP there was a fledgling security service consisting of a small force of detectives organised in 1864 by then Premier of the Province of Canada and later the country's first prime minister, Sir John A. Macdonald. This agency was largely concerned with the US Civil War and sought to protect Canada from incursions from the US side to punish Canada for failing to maintain neutrality in the war. With the end of conflict in April 1865, however, this threat dissipated.

A force known as the Dominion Police was created by the fledgling federal government in 1868 to guard the Parliament Buildings in Ottawa following the assassination of Thomas D'Arcy McGee by an Irish Fenian (see next chapter). It had a "Secret Service" section that took advantage of the detectives and agents referred to in the previous paragraph. According to Horrall, the Secret Service, under Canada's first "intelligence chief," Gilbert McMicken, "used paid informers, intercepted telegraph messages, and opened mail in order to create an effective security system . . . the Prime Minister was closely informed of all operations."

After the Fenian threat had faded away—although a lock of the Welland Canal was dynamited by suspected Irish American terrorists as late as 1900—the Secret Service did provide bodyguards for visiting royalty and "noted the movements" of international anarchists. This reflects what US academic David Rapoport calls the first wave of terrorism (i.e., the "anarchist wave") that dominated from the late 19th into the early 20th centuries. For example, in 1901 to 1902, the Secret Service received rumours that a US-based secret organisation known as the Order of the Midnight Sun was planning to seize Yukon (in northwestern Canada) by force.[6] Nothing came of the plot.

During World War I, the Secret Service was occupied with the presence of "alien foreigners" in Canada, largely German immigrants but also Slavs who fell under the yoke of Austro-Hungarian Empire. My own maternal grandfather, who was Ukrainian but held an Austro-Hungarian passport, was believed, or so my mother told me, to have been picked up and incarcerated in a "work camp" in Quebec during that war.

After the scare of the Winnipeg General Strike in 1919 and alarm over Bolshevik conspiracies, the NWMP absorbed the Dominion Police Force and the two became the RCMP in 1920.

With the creation of the Ontario Provincial Police (OPP) in 1909, driven by the need to keep law and order in the northern part of the province (and hence very far from Toronto) in the wake of mining booms, and the Sûreté du Québec (SQ) in 1930 (a merger of provincial police forces in Québec City and Montreal), the policing landscape became complicated. In addition to these two forces, we must include the hundreds of municipal ones.

Generally speaking, the RCMP is responsible for national security across Canada from a law enforcement perspective, but it also carries out regular policing duties in eight provinces, three territories and innumerable towns and cities through what is known as contract policing: this is less germane to our analysis. It should be noted, however, that the OPP did create its own provincial security arm, the Provincial Anti-Terrorism Section (OPP-PATS) in 2002, for which I worked as an advisor in 2015.

For much of its early history the RCMP was concerned first and foremost with day-to-day policing matters. There was a national security section, but this appears to have dealt mostly with foreign espionage (i.e., CI investigations), a file that took on more importance with the defection of cipher clerk Igor Gouzenko from the Soviet Embassy in Ottawa shortly after the end of World War II (and seen by some as the true launch of the Cold War). It should be noted, then, that the Communist threat (also known as the "red scare") was the RCMP's national security intelligence priority during the 1920s and 1930s. During World War II itself, German and Italian Canadians were again interned as perceived wartime threats to Canadian national security, much akin to what happened during World War I, as were fascists.

The bureaus within the RCMP with primary responsibility for national security issues were the Criminal Investigation Branch (CIB) and the Special Branch (SB), created in 1950. Concerns were expressed by some that Canada would go down the path of McCarthyism and start spying flagrantly on Canadians, especially those in trade unions, and teachers or professors. The Special Branch became the Directorate of Security and Intelligence in 1962, and finally the RCMP Security Service in 1970 (following yet another Canadian Royal Commission: we do a lot of these).

Following the FLQ crisis in Quebec in the 1970s (to be discussed at much greater length in Chapter 2), and allegations of improper conduct by the Security Service, the government of Canada decided to strike a body (known as the McDonald Commission) to look into these issues. The Commission issued its final report in 1981 and for our purposes the most significant recommendation was to create a civilian security intelligence agency. This recommendation was accepted, and the Canadian Security Intelligence Service, known in Ottawa as "the Service," saw the light of day in July 1984.

I spoke at great length with a former CSIS colleague who worked on the committees and in government offices responsible for looking at the McDonald Commission report and drafting legislation that led to the creation of CSIS. Indeed, this person had a front row seat during a multi-year process, and offered me fascinating insights into long meetings, a wealth of consultation among many government departments, and the care with which the process unfolded. Those given the task of sculpting a new civilian security intelligence service were well aware of the need to carefully weigh civil liberties and freedoms while also ensuring that national security and public safety were safeguarded. As it was explained to me, then Solicitor General Robert Kaplan expressed that a specialised organisation was required to respond to the increasingly sophisticated nature of threats to our security. Explanatory notes from the office of the Solicitor General regarding the creation of CSIS reflect this, and quote the Mackenzie Commission (1969), which noted:

> We all recognise that dealing with the matter of security is a difficult one indeed because there are two principles which must be reconciled. The task of Parliament, and certainly the task of government, is to find a balance between these two principles. The first principle, of course, is that the government is charged with the responsibility of maintaining the security and integrity of the State against subversion, and any efforts on the part of those who seek to change our society by resorting to force. . . . But against that lies another principle, that we must guarantee the rights of the individual so that under the guise of security no person can receive unfair treatment.[7]

Note the use of the term *subversion*: the phrase "political violence and terrorism" was also used in the early discussions. Interestingly, there was concern over the definition of subversion but not for the definition of terrorism. This had to do with the delicate balance between legitimate dissent and subversion as it related to the new security service's investigation of the activities of Canadian citizens. After much debate, the wording that was settled on was: "Activities directed toward the disruption by covertly committed criminal means or directed toward or intended ultimately to lead to the destruction or overthrow of the democratic system of government in Canada." Not that the government wanted a purely security intelligence organisation to investigate overt criminal acts (that is the responsibility of law enforcement agencies).

In response to concerns that CSIS would investigate "Canadians supporting the Afghan rebels" (recall that this is shortly after the Soviet invasion of Afghanistan in late 1979), civil servants prepared the following response:

> As law abiding and freedom-loving Canadians, we may well support: both the aims and the methods of the Afghan rebels; the aims but certainly not some of the methods of the IRA, and; neither the aims nor the methods of groups such as the Red Brigade. What these examples demonstrate is the difficulty in trying to draw a distinction in statute between what I may call "good violence" and "bad" violence—an acceptable level or form of violence and unacceptable level or form of violence—violence which we can support and violence which we do not support.[8]

It was even suggested that "the throwing of a tomato at a political figure" could be construed as "the threat or use of violence for the purpose of achieving a political objective."[9] The government countered by adding "serious" before "violence" in section 2 (c) and added that lawful advocacy, protest, and dissent would remain acceptable in Canada.

Some of these objections may seem frivolous in hindsight. Who would seriously worry that a tomato tosser would he seen as a terrorist? It does speak, however, to several understandable concerns. Recall that the idea behind creating CSIS stemmed from the findings that its predecessor, the RCMP Security Service, had engaged in illegal activities. There were doubtless those who were convinced that this new civilian spy agency would go back to the 'same old, same old', especially given that most of the workforce would be ex-Mounties who traded in their red serge for a suit and tie. There are still those who maintain that CSIS engages in illegal activities thirty-eight years later!

There were also concerns that a civilian agency would exercise powers not consistent with a democracy. There are far too many examples of such organisations around the world, mostly in non-democracies, which are the eyes and ears (and "enforcers") of the party in power, and not a neutral state agency tasked with national security investigations. Concerned Canadians—or at least some of them—were merely expressing legitimate fears and exercising their rights in a democratic state.

Many Canadian lobby groups sought to influence and amend the legislation and many of these were the usual cast of characters: civil liberties organisations, provincial attorneys general, teachers' unions, and the like (even the Coalition for Gay Rights in Ontario). At the end of the day the legislation received royal assent (albeit the original bill, C-157 was withdrawn and redrafted as C-9) in the Senate on June 26, 1984. CSIS was born three weeks later.

When CSIS opened its doors, those RCMP officers working in the Security Service were offered a choice: keep their commission and be reassigned within the Force or resign and join CSIS as a civilian. Those who opted to join CSIS were also offered a two-year window during which they could return to the RCMP should they so decide. Many took the latter option and the new agency also began to hire Canadians and train them to be intelligence officers, responsible for carrying out national security investigations. As a result, the very early days of the civilian agency were heavily influenced by ex-RCMP officers, as predicted by those who saw the creation of CSIS as nothing more than a paper exercise.

I spoke with many individuals who made the switch in 1984. They all told me that the choice was an easy one. A life in the RCMP entails movement across the country as the Force is indeed a national one. A posting to CSIS meant that some could settle down in Ottawa, although CSIS too is a national service

One of my contacts who was in the first civilian cohort of intelligence officers told me that, upon being hired, they were told that they were the "new generation" and that the former RCMP members would be gone "in a couple of years." That clearly did not happen.

There is also much to be said about the birth of CSIS out of the former RCMP Security Service. It should not come as a total surprise that many at the RCMP were not happy to see a new agency usurp some of its functions which, after all, it (in its various forms) had held since before Confederation. As a result, cooperation was not the greatest at the beginning. That has changed significantly, as many of my contacts, both from CSIS and the RCMP, have told me. Nevertheless, the first CSIS HQ, located in what was known as the East Memorial Building across from the Supreme Court of Canada in Ottawa, left a lot to be desired when it came to structural integrity and comfort. When CSIS moved to its new central command in the eastern part of the city in the mid-1990s all were much happier.

Of course, the advent of CSIS did not take the RCMP out of the national security game. The two organisations have very different mandates, aside from the obvious police-civilian one. CSIS collects intelligence on threats to national security as outlined in section 2 of the CSIS Act and can do so on a "reasonable grounds to suspect" basis. The four areas outlined in that section of the Act are:

a) espionage or sabotage that is against Canada or is detrimental to the interests of Canada or activities directed toward or in support of such espionage or sabotage,

b) foreign influenced activities within or relating to Canada that are detrimental to the interests of Canada and are clandestine or deceptive or involve a threat to any person,

c) activities within or relating to Canada directed toward or in support of the threat or use of acts of serious violence against persons or property for the purpose of achieving a political, religious or ideological objective within Canada or a foreign state, and

d) activities directed toward undermining by covert unlawful acts, or directed toward or intended ultimately to lead to the destruction or overthrow by violence of, the constitutionally established system of government in Canada.

In this book only matters concerning section 2 (c) will be considered.

The other important part of the CSIS mandate relevant to our discussion is section 12: "The Service shall collect, by investigation or otherwise, to the extent that it is strictly necessary, and analyse and retain information and intelligence respecting activities that may on reasonable grounds be suspected of constituting threats to the security of Canada and, in relation thereto, shall report to and advise the Government of Canada."

This section gives CSIS its authority to undertake national security investigations. I want to focus on the words "shall report to and advise." CSIS has no powers of arrest. It is a collector of intelligence and it shares that intelligence with other government agencies. Most Canadians see the organisation as overly secretive. While that is true to a large extent, there is a great deal that is indeed given to appropriate government bodies with a "need to know." As one contact told me, "briefing up is in our (i.e., CSIS's) DNA."

For its part, the RCMP collects evidence to be used in possible prosecutions and does so on a "reasonable grounds to believe" basis. In Canada intelligence proper is not the same as evidence and cannot be used in a court of law: CSIS does not want its secret sources and methods to be made public (although sources can agree to "cross the floor" and become RCMP assets, as has happened in several high-profile counterterrorism cases). Both organisations can apply for federal court intercept warrants, deploy human intelligence gatherers (sources in CSIS parlance and agents in the RCMP's), and use physical surveillance.

These differences between the two organisations—evidence vs. intelligence, uniformed vs. civilian, "suspect" vs. "believe"—were recognised early in the deliberations that led to the creation of CSIS.

While CSIS information is not collected to further judicial proceedings, it can be shared, in a minimal manner, with the RCMP. This exchange is performed to assist the RCMP in its independent work and is carried out in a way that does not compromise CSIS sources or methods. The tools that enable this exchange are called disclosure and advisory letters: the former is a way to provide the RCMP with very basic information upon which an investigative lead can begin, that is, when CSIS is of the opinion that criminal activity is taking place (or close to taking place), while the latter is the provision of actual intelligence which both agencies acknowledge may go to court. Neither tool was mentioned in the CSIS Act and they came out of an awareness that there had to be a more effective way to work toward the same goal of keeping Canadians safe.

CSIS and the RCMP do not engage in "joint" operations for reasons already discussed—they may, however, carry out "parallel" investigations. For instance, CSIS may decide to continue looking at individuals tied to someone who is the subject of an RCMP criminal probe, for reasons of further intelligence gathering. In my experience the relationship, while not perfect, works well in a Canadian setting. The two organisations do have a joint management team as well as an executive management team, both of which are in place to ensure that the two agencies can work together as well as possible, keeping in mind the need to not interfere in law enforcement cases that may end up in Canadian courts. The recognition that there was always room for improvements led to the launching of what became known as One Vision in the early 2010s.

I also saw many counterterrorism investigations in Canada that began as CSIS operations before some (not all) were handed off to the RCMP.

There are several reasons for this. As noted, CSIS has a lower threshold of investigative power (reasonable grounds to suspect vs. the RCMP's reasonable grounds to believe). The RCMP takes an interest when there is enough information to suggest that further investigation could lead to criminal charges, arrest, and prosecution. It is my understanding that many of the terrorism cases that eventually were brought to light began at CSIS or with CSIS input. It also bears repeating that the RCMP mandate is much larger in scope than that of CSIS (refer to the four parts listed above as section 2 of the CSIS Act). The RCMP has to look at all matters of a criminal nature, not just terrorism.

There are also many, many investigations that do not end up in court. Some are valid for "background" reasons. Others may lead to additional individuals who themselves may be charged under the Canadian Criminal Code. CSIS does not look at anyone randomly: there have to be reasonable grounds. In my experience, every single person on whom some level of effort was expended was rightly examined, and many investigations were relatively quickly dropped once it was clear that there was no "there" there. These people were not strictly speaking innocent—they may not have been guilty in a legal sense, but they were most definitely involved in activities of concern. As one contact told me, "How dirty does a shirt have to be before you say it's dirty?" In the words of another contact, "there are varying levels of badness."

On the issue of CSIS's targeting of those who never ended up "doing anything," a note of clarification may be useful here. As mentioned, under its legislation CSIS is specialized to investigate threats to national security (defined in section 2 of the CSIS Act) where it has reasonable grounds to suspect a threat is present. This constitutes a lower threshold than the "reasonable grounds to believe" that constrains law enforcement in Canada. In essence, CSIS has the ability to get an earlier look at what is being planned.

It was my experience while working at CSIS that the vast majority of investigations never led to any actual act planned (which would have been passed on to the RCMP for their further action). In other words, most people who "talk the talk" never "walk the walk." This is just human nature I suppose, since words are easier to pronounce than actions are to implement.

Some would argue that CSIS was in effect looking at people who were never going to pose a threat in the first place, and that this was somehow a violation of their Charter rights. Nothing could be further from the truth.

We should want organisations like CSIS to do the initial legwork on possible threats and to weed out the wannabes from the real McCoys. Having all this put on the shoulders of agencies such as the RCMP gives these organisations far too much additional work, and they are already overtaxed and oversubscribed. When CSIS discloses information to the RCMP it lets the latter know that, yes, a serious threat does exist, and that law enforcement action may be necessary to collect evidence with a view to laying charges. In addition, it is the RCMP, and not CSIS, that has the mandate to stop acts of terrorism from materializing.

I am under no illusion that this attempt to explain why CSIS does what it does will satisfy everyone. I am aware that for some Canadians CSIS is the devil incarnate no matter what it does or does not do. For individuals who hold to those beliefs, nothing I say or write will make a whit of difference.

As a national force, the RCMP has a lot on its plate. Divided into divisions across the country, some parts of Canada would not see many (if any) terrorism cases. Nevertheless, as one of my RCMP contacts told me, there was no pushback from regions when an unexpected terrorism case arose. The required resources would be allocated and taken from another region if necessary.

In larger counterterrorism investigations, the RCMP can also avail itself of the Integrated National Security Enforcement Teams (INSETS), created after 9/11 to better ensure information sharing across agencies at various levels of government. These are agencies composed of representatives of the RCMP, federal partners and agencies, as well as provincial and municipal police services. This specialized team collects, analyses, and shares intelligence in order to detect, investigate, and disrupt terrorist groups or individuals who pose a threat to Canada's national security. As of 2020 there are five INSETs, in Ottawa, Montreal, Toronto, Edmonton, and Vancouver. In recent years, terrorism arrests have been announced by a given INSET following one of its investigations.

According to an RCMP contact, earlier versions of integrated teams had demonstrated that collaboration works. It was always better to have more agencies involved, as it was a "win, win, win all around." The RCMP benefitted greatly from the bringing together of the knowledge and experiences of participating agencies, including, for example, the Canada

Border Services Agency (CBSA). Local partners knew their backyards and made important contributions to counterterrorism investigations. Other Government of Canada agencies also took on counterterrorism responsibilities, though not all wisely in my opinion. I would assume the same happened in other nations.

Taking all this into consideration, my 32-year career gave me direct access to CSIS and OPP-PATS information and indirect access to RCMP and INSET holdings. Hence, those organisations will feature in the chapters to come. For the record, the CSE I worked for in the 1980s and 1990s did not do counterterrorism much. It is my understanding that changed in the post 9/11 period, a time during which I moved from CSE to CSIS. In light of my lack of visibility of CSE's counterterrorism capabilities today, I will not make much reference to that agency in this book.

Mention must also be made of intelligence shared with Canadian agencies by its partners and allies. CSIS and the RCMP have robust relationships with many federal, provincial, territorial, and municipal partners across Canada which can assist with information gathered in keeping with their own jurisdictions, mandates, and powers. On many occasions this assistance has been invaluable. There are robust mechanisms to share information. Many think that not enough is shared and there is some truth to this. Nevertheless, the sensitivity of certain types of intelligence necessitates close handling and limited distribution.

Canada also benefits enormously from its international allies. Two such groups warrant special mention. Since the aftermath of World War II, the so-called "Five Eyes" club has constituted perhaps the greatest multinational intelligence arrangement in history. Agencies from Australia, Canada, New Zealand, the UK, and the US exchange raw and finished intelligence on a daily basis. This includes both SIGINT and HUMINT.

In addition, CSIS and the RCMP enter into memoranda of understanding with their counterparts in hundreds of nations around the world. At CSIS this facility is managed under section 17 of the CSIS Act. During my time at CSIS regular conversations with security intelligence services outside the Five Eyes were invaluable to our understanding of the international terrorism threat. In many investigations timely intelligence shared with Canada was critical to counterterrorism investigations. Some were very adept at understanding the Islamist extremism threat—the Netherlands, Denmark, Australia, the UK, France, Germany and the

Scandinavian countries come to mind.

Sharing with the intelligence and security services of nations that have different systems of governance and different "rules of the game" is of course fraught with challenges. I will return to these issues in the penultimate chapter.

When it comes to the most important relationship, that between CSIS and the RCMP, an RCMP contact confided that when it came to counterterrorism the relationship was "excellent." Trust levels were high and CSIS was very open with senior RCMP officials. At the same time, discussions on disclosures (i.e., the sharing of intelligence) were not always easy. Deconfliction was handled well, that is, both agencies made sure to the extent possible that resources were well deployed.

Investigations were complicated on occasion by short time frames. There were instances where information was shared on potential threats without enough time or space to carry out adequate investigations ("it was hard to get up to speed"). In the end, all of these issues were dealt with on a case-by-case basis. Having CSIS staff within INSETs was a clear advantage.

It is also worth pointing out that when a counterterrorism investigation works well, when all cylinders are firing, sometimes nothing happens. No one is arrested. No court cases ensue. I recall one case that involved a suspicious incident on a transportation chokepoint in a Canadian city. Eyewitnesses reported two individuals acting in a way that raised alarm. Those witnesses worked with law enforcement to create a composite drawing and that image was recognised by an officer. The individual in the drawing was approached, information was gathered, and a potential threat was neutralised. No muss, no fuss. Case closed. Nothing was made public and no repercussions ever arose. Canadians of course are in the dark about this incident, and the lack of reflection in open fora may contribute to a general ignorance of the nature of the terrorist menace in this country.

It is also important to stress that counterterrorism was not always the top priority at CSIS. At its creation CSIS was still very much a CI organization, focused on following foreign spies in Canada. Several contacts, including former directors, stressed that the investigations in the beginning were predominantly CI, not CT, ones. There was a "learning curve" that needed to be mastered—as it turns out very quickly in light of the Air India attack in July 1985. I am not trying to give the impression that there were no counterterrorism efforts, but rather to emphasise that CI was seen as the more important task: this indeed was a holdover from the RCMP Security Service days. The shift toward a greater counterterrorism effort began to occur after Air India, as other plots involving Sikh terrorists in Canada, some of whom were seeking to plan attacks in India itself, came to light. As the Islamist terrorist threat gathered strength, more resources were dedicated to counterterrorism.

Terrorist Listings

Another part of Canada's judicial management of terrorist offences was the creation of a "listed terrorist entities" regime. This is used to identify groups that are considered terrorist in nature and for which any facilitation is considered an offence. The list is kept by Public Safety Canada (PSC). On its website PSC notes:

> The listing of an entity is a public means of identifying a group or individual as being associated with terrorism. The definition of an entity includes a person, group, trust, partnership or fund, or an unincorporated association or organisation. It is not a crime to be listed. However, one of the consequences of being listed is that the entity's property can be the subject of seizure/restraint and/or forfeiture. In addition, institutions such as banks, brokerages, etc. are subject to reporting requirements with respect to an entity's property and must not allow those entities to access the property. These institutions may not deal or otherwise dispose of the property. It is an offence to knowingly participate in or contribute to, directly or indirectly, any activity of a terrorist group. This participation is only an offence if its purpose is to enhance the ability of any terrorist group to facilitate or carry out a terrorist activity. The process of listing begins with criminal and/or security intelligence reports on an entity disclosing the reasonable grounds to believe that the entity has knowingly carried out, attempted to carry out, participated in or facilitated a terrorist activity; or the entity is knowingly acting on behalf of, at the direction of or in association with, an entity involved in a terrorist activity. The criminal and/or security intelligence reports are submitted to the Minister of Public Safety for consideration. If the Minister has reasonable grounds to believe that the above test is met, the Minister may make a recommendation to the Governor in Council to place the entity on the list.[10]

In the Appendix the reader will find the list of entities current to

January, 2023. Many of these entities will feature in later chapters.

The lists may be based on intelligence, but the publicly available summaries must obviously be based on open-source information. I am blind to the current process of where these summaries are composed now, but I recall contributing to the initial effort to compile such a list.

In the aftermath of 9/11, it was decided that Canada needed to make it illegal, for all intents and purposes, to belong to a terrorist entity. In order to do so, it needed to ascertain which groups were indeed terrorist groups. The first attempt to do this was assigned to CSIS in 2002, to the analysis branch where I worked. Teams of analysts were each given a group to research and summarise using open-source information: one of the entities that was my responsibility was Al Qaeda. Once we had drafted our summaries, legal teams at CSIS went through them with a view to ensuring they were accurate and would withstand a court challenge (in the event Usama bin Laden sued Canada?).

According to one contact, CSIS was merely following in the footsteps of the United Nations when it elected (or more likely was instructed) to create the list. The decision not to use intelligence, while understandable in that a public document had to be open, was seen as a hindrance. After all, there was lots of secret information on AQ and other groups, so why not include it? In addition, there were questions about expending time and resources to list an entity that had no activity in Canada.

To my knowledge this list has been rarely used in Canadian courts to point to terrorist membership or support. Nevertheless, it remains a tool to support the spirit of Canada's anti-terrorism legislation. Interestingly, in September 2020 the highly respected Combating Terrorism Center at West Point issued a paper on the US versions of terrorist and terrorist entity lists, in which the authors stated that the broader efficacy of both lists is unclear at best and that they are, on some level, political tools, adding that "despite the increasing use of both tools, little work has been done to understand the impact of these programs."[11]

Note as well that the vast majority of the listed entities are Islamist extremist in nature. In fact, when Blood and Honour, and Combat 18 were added in June 2019 it made big news in Canada and was paraded as if the government had finally recognised far-right terrorism as real.

A January 2021 decision by the Trudeau government to consider listing the Proud Boys in the wake of the riot at the US Capitol in Washington led to the first real public debate on the listing process. For what it is worth, I weighed in that this tool is highly political and of little operational use.[12] In this I agree with the West Point paper.

With this overview completed it is time to turn to actual acts of terrorism in Canada and abroad.

2

Ethno-Nationalist Terrorism in Canada

With the first dawn of this gladsome midsummer morn, we hail the birthday of a new nationality. A united British America, with its four millions of people, takes its place this day among the nations of the world. Let us hope that Canadians—using the word in its new and large acceptation—will worthily fulfil the duties which Providence has confided to them.
                              - Editorial from The Globe newspaper July 1, 1867

Just watch me.
                              - Canadian Prime Minister Pierre E. Trudeau, 1970 October Crisis

IN THIS CHAPTER, WE WILL EXAMINE TERRORISTS and terrorist groups that planned and carried out acts of terrorism in Canada in furtherance of nationalist or ethnic goals and movements. Some of the acts were small while some were so large as to be catastrophic in nature.

Definition

What do I mean by *nationalist terrorism*? Simply put, these are actions executed by groups of people who self-identify as an ethnic entity. In most cases, these entities believe that their sense of identity is hampered, thwarted or even forbidden by another entity (often a state). In some cases, terrorist groups are seeking recognition of a historical wrong and have opted to use violence against the perceived party responsible for that wrong. In the most serious instances, this violence is deployed to force a state to grant autonomy or independence to an ethnic group.

By making this distinction I contrast this form of terrorism with what has been termed *religious terrorism*, that is, largely Islamist—the subject of the next chapter. This should not insinuate that there is no religious aspect to certain forms of nationalist terrorism, for example Sikh terrorism, which is a point discussed in my last book, *When Religion Kills*. It is always difficult to pigeonhole violent extremism since perpetrators often (usually?) are influenced by multiple factors. This should not hamper our discussion.

Canada has become a multiethnic nation, with much of its diversity accelerating in the post–World War II period. What was once largely a British and French country, in addition to the original First Nations inhabitants, has transformed into one of the world's most multicultural polities. And while this transformation has not always been smooth, Canada is nevertheless seen by other nations as a success story: this is evidenced by the hundreds of thousands of people who seek to migrate here every year. Many foreign governments seek to learn how this country achieved this reality.

Canadians generally enthusiastically support immigration and that, too, is somewhat rare in our world. Still, along with the import of peoples from so many cultural, linguistic, and religious backgrounds has come the import of grievances. Canada has thus become the arena in which overseas battles have played out, sometimes with tragic results.

The five main terrorist movements to be discussed in this chapter in chronological order are: Irish nationalist extremism, French Canadian nationalism, Armenian genocide retribution groups, Sikh extremists, and Iranians opposed to the regime of the ayatollahs. There may be others (the Liberation Tigers of Tamil Eelam, investigated under the rubric of terrorist financing and logistics support, comes immediately to mind) but none have succeeded in carrying out any acts of terrorism on Canadian soil.

Irish Nationalist Terrorism

The story of Canada's rise to nationhood is a (relatively) peaceful one. Yes, there were isolated acts of violence by those who wanted to cut ties to Great Britain, but this country never found itself in a war of independence like its neighbour to the south, the United States. As a child I recall learning in school about the "rebellions" in Upper and Lower Canada—neither amounted to much. As a student at the University of Western Ontario ((UWO), now known more simply as Western University) I sat in on one history professor's satire of the insurrection led by William Lyon McKenzie in 1837.

No, Canada almost came softly into its own in July 1867 and the notion that it is a fairly calm land is reflected in section 91 of the former British North America Act (now called the Constitution Act), describing the power to make laws for the "peace, order and good government." This compares rather meekly to the *liberté, égalité, fraternité* of the French Revolution or the American "life, liberty and the pursuit of happiness" found in that nation's Constitution.

Canada was different and is seen by many, at least in my experience, as somewhat of a role model internationally. Millions have emigrated here to make a new life and Canada, with a few exceptions, has remained open to newcomers. A little more than a quarter century after Confederation, then

Prime Minister Wilfrid Laurier famously proclaimed, "the 20th century belongs to Canada."

He was a little off in that boast.

Even if Canada did not "own" the 20th (or 21st) century, it turned out to be a fairly good place to live (the climate notwithstanding!). Without ignoring shameful policies and actions toward Canadian First Nations over the decades, we are not plagued with the levels of violence seen in the US with its Second Amendment "right to bear arms" and astronomical rates of gun ownership and shootings. We do not have anywhere near the number of gang deaths seen in parts of Central America and elsewhere. Organised crime is here—of that is no doubt—but crime syndicates do not run our cities. We have not had a war on our soil, save for the US-instigated War of 1812: no civil strife, no occupation, no real threat from outside forces. Canada is, for all intents and purposes, the "peaceable kingdom."

And yet the promise of that midsummer day in 1867 was shattered less than a year later.

Thomas D'Arcy McGee, a Father of Confederation

There is a small plaque on a non-descript office building in Ottawa's downtown core, a block or two south of Parliament Hill. It is easy to miss and I imagine that a lot of Ottawans are unaware of its existence. The English version of the bilingual inscription reads as follows (as all things federal in Canada, the sign is in English and French):

> Journalist, poet, Irish patriot, Canadian statesman and Father of Confederation, McGee was born in Ireland, where he was involved in nationalist politics. Forced to flee to America in 1848, he worked for several years in the United States before settling in Montréal in 1857. In 1858 he was first elected to the legislature for Montréal West. An eloquent orator in support of Confederation, McGee attended the Charlottetown and Québec Conferences, and later represented Montréal West in the House of Commons until felled near this site by an assassin's bullet on April 7, 1868.

A second plaque on a building in downtown Ottawa named after Thomas D'Arcy McGee also mentions the terrorist act of 1868.

The assassination of Thomas D'Arcy McGee was arguably Canada's first successful terrorist attack. Let us look at this incident.

In the run up to Canadian independence in 1867 a few figures loom large. They were all men, this being the 19th century after all. And none loomed as large as Thomas D'Arcy McGee. My children attended one of the many schools, primary and secondary, named after him. There is also a fine pub located in Ottawa less than a block from where he met his end.

Born in Ireland in 1825, McGee was originally a staunch supporter of Irish nationalism and liberation—he joined the Young Ireland Movement and even tried to raise the fire of rebellion in northeast Ireland. This failed and caught the eye of the British, forcing him to return to the US in 1848, where he had lived since 1842.

McGee was originally keen to establish an Irish colony in the western part of the US or Canada and his passion earned him the nickname "Moses McGee." He fought with powerful anti-Irish forces in the US, the self-styled "Know Nothings," as well as influential Catholic leaders in New York, and after his failed colony plan, he emigrated to Montreal in 1857.

He became involved in politics and was elected as one of three Montreal representatives to the Province of Canada's Legislative Assembly. He was now a Canadian in support of Canada as a separate nation, and increasingly saw the benefits of the British constitutional monarchy, in essence a reversal of his previous Irish independence bias. He attended both the Charlottetown and Quebec Conferences in 1864, two landmark events that led to Confederation in 1867.

McGee later made the critical mistake of voicing criticism of the Fenians, an Irish nationalist movement, and was hence seen as a traitor to the movement. In the early hours of Tuesday, April 7, 1868, McGee was assassinated outside his Ottawa home near the current Sparks Street, a block from Parliament Hill. Authorities suspected a Fenian conspiracy and swiftly arrested Patrick James Whelan, who maintained his innocence throughout his trial and was never proven to be a Fenian. Police did find Irish nationalist literature in the hotel room where he was staying as well as a gun that had been recently fired. Witnesses claimed that Whelan had said on several occasions that he wanted to kill McGee. In the end, he was convicted of murder and hanged before more than five thousand onlookers on February 11, 1869. The location of his execution, the former Carleton County Jail (also known as the Nicholas Street Gaol or simply the Ottawa Jail) still stands in the central part of the city, although it now functions as a youth hostel. Whelan was one of the last to suffer a public hanging in.

The funeral of Thomas D'Arcy McGee in Montreal attracted tens of thousands. He is remembered today as an advocate for minority rights in

Canada. That he was once a stalwart supporter of Irish independence from England and was killed by an alleged violent advocate of the same is ironic, although his political shift in favour of the British constitutional monarchy was seen by many as treason.

Not surprisingly, I was unable to interview anyone who worked the Fenian file or who investigated McGee's assassination. In this respect, the very first terrorist attack in Canadian history will be treated in this book apart from all the others. It says something that Canada went almost a century between its first and second terrorist attacks.

Wait, Who Were the Fenians?

McGee's alleged killer, Patrick Whelan, was labelled a Fenian sympathiser. The Fenians were a loosely organised Irish movement, a secret society founded in 1858 after the failed uprising in 1848, and the catastrophic potato famine (which they blamed on England), which sought to win an independent Ireland from the United Kingdom. They were active in the 19th and early 20th centuries in Ireland, England, the US, and, most importantly for our purposes, in Canada. The name "Fenians" stems from "Fianna"—a band of legendary Irish warriors. In this, the Fenians were similar to many violent extremist groups which see their inspiration in a past, either real or mythical.

The Irish diasporas in North America were active in raising funds and awareness of the struggle back in Ireland. This of course made sense as there was mass migration to the new world by survivors of the famine who made the trip in what became known as "coffin ships," on account of the high fatality rates on the voyage. Canada, in particular, was seen as a high value target for Irish nationalists because until mid-1867 it was a UK colony. An infamous Fenian raid took place in the Niagara Peninsula in June 1866 and incurred a response by the British-Canadian militia in what has been called the Battle of Ridgeway. There were other raids in New Brunswick and Quebec as late as 1871.

Given that the uniqueness of this book is to hear the first-hand experiences of Canadians who worked in counterterrorism, it is of course impossible to do so for this particular act as it occurred 150-plus years ago and there is no one still living from that era. I was very fortunate, however, to strike up a conversation with Canada's foremost specialist on the Fenians, University of Toronto professor David Wilson. In an undated paper found in Library and Archives Canada, Professor Wilson stated that the Fenians were "very much a minority" in Irish Catholic Canada, counting on no more than 3,000 "members" out of a total population of 250,000. Further, those who actively supported an invasion from the US were a minority of a minority. In his words "they were of marginal importance, and the Fenian scare was exaggerated to the point of paranoia."

Nevertheless, there were Fenian brotherhoods in most Canadian urban centres and Professor Wilson believes they punched above their weight. They never came close to their stated goal of achieving Irish independence, but they were of concern to British and Canadian security authorities.

I had a long discussion with Professor Wilson in June 2020,[13] and the bulk of this section is derived from his comments during that conversation, with direct quotes from him duly noted.

One of the reasons the Fenians took to terrorism was a realisation born out of the failed 1848 uprising that Britain was simply too powerful to defeat militarily (as Wilson said, "it was futile, counterproductive, and must be opposed"). Another was the notion that fighting Britain had to be done more smartly, through the creation of a secret organisation (hence, the Fenians). Nationalists also hoped that England would become enmeshed in a European war which would divert its attention and open it up to attacks.

The lack of a European war led to a scenario where perhaps England and the US would go to war, as they had in 1812. Fenians had largely given up on attacks in Ireland itself as the UK secret service was too efficient and had crushed any such possibility. But, they felt that if Irish Americans were to engage in incursions into Canada with the tacit approval of the US government, then England would retaliate, thus taking its attention away from what was happening in Ireland. There was also an element of revenge: the Fenians saw Canada and England as synonymous: after all the Union Jack did fly over Canada. In Professor Wilson's words, Canada was a "sitting duck" for incursions.

The new Canadian secret service was taken by surprise by the 1866 raid in Niagara by a force of between 800 and 1,000 Fenians who were met by a hastily formed militia that included students from the University of Toronto. The Canadian side was badly outmanned by the Fenians, many of whom were US Civil War veterans and a dozen or so Canadians were killed before a retreat was ordered. When the regular British army advanced the Fenians elected to retreat, in part as their planned three-pronged attack had failed to materialise.

Nevertheless, the attack was enthusiastically celebrated in Fenian and Irish nationalist circles: it was seen as a victory where "the boys in green defeated the boys in red." It also served to convince the terrorists that the idea of germinating an England-US war was not a bad idea. In the end the American government was not that supportive and only declared some backing in order to secure the American Irish vote.

Despite the lack of success, the threat could have been worse. Even if the Fenians had no realistic chance of taking over Canada they did hold to the notion that they would be welcomed, or at least not opposed, by both French and Irish Catholics. "They were strong enough to do significant economic damage," largely through the costs incurred by having to continually call out the militia. Had they been able to hold territory for a week, there could have been an upswelling of support from other Irish Americans who were not Fenians.

When asking whether the Fenians were freedom fighters or terrorists, the matter of perspective is of course important. They clearly saw themselves as freedom fighters, while McGee saw them as immoral and irreligious, and although he did not use the actual word "terrorism" he did note that they "sowed terror among peaceable Canadians" and had no justification for what they were doing.

Sixteen of the Fenians captured at Ridgway were tried, convicted, and given death sentences. The UK was "horrified" that any of them would be executed as that would make them martyrs, and the British government made this clear to Canada. In the end, Canada followed UK advice and commuted the sentences to long prison sentences.

For his part, McGee gave a speech in November 1866 in Montreal, a "Fenian hotbed," in which he said, "these men deserve death." As for his later assassin, while we will never know for certain that Patrick Whelan was indeed a Fenian, there was substantial circumstantial evidence that he was (at a minimum he was a sympathiser, if not a sworn secret member). Surprisingly, McGee's murder was not an authorised Fenian hit: the Fenians did have an assassination squad in Dublin but not in New York (their headquarters in America). Nevertheless, Whelan hated McGee and was heard to publicly voice a wish to see him dead. Whelan did go up to McGee's house in Ottawa on two occasions with the intention of assassinating him before he did so in April 1868.

Implications of This Terrorist Act

McGee remains the only Canadian federal politician to have been felled by an assassin—in this case a terrorist affiliated with Irish nationalism and independence from Britain. Interestingly, a Canadian prime minister found himself in a Centre Block caucus room metres away from another terrorist attack in October 2014, but more on that later.

There are several aspects to this incident which warrant comment. Firstly, the violent push for Irish independence gained impetus toward the end of World War I and is a prime example of what the American academic David Rapoport calls the second wave of terrorism in his wave theory. That Canada was the scene of a terrorist act of this nature a full half century before Irish nationalism became energised is interesting in my view.

Secondly, the Fenian threat never amounted to much, as the discussion above illustrates. Canada, it would seem, was not viewed as an important enough terrain to engage in this struggle for independence. Other countries, such as Ireland and the UK, would later prove to be ground zero for this terrorist campaign.

Thirdly, the fact that an act of terrorism tied to a grievance that had nothing to do with Canada took place here is important. As we shall see, many other attacks would be planned and executed in this country seeking to draw attention to foreign disputes and to use Canada as a stage.

Fourthly, even if the Fenians faded away quickly and left no significant impact on the Canadian scene some of their heirs (for example, the Irish Republican Army (IRA) and its variations) were active in the 1970s and 1980s. Professor Wilson went so far as to say that the Fenians were the IRA in the 1860s. He added that there were intelligence reports showing that Irish Canadians in Montreal during World War I were willing to team up with Germans to target British interests in Canada, although this went nowhere.

In my interviews with several former RCMP Security Service and later CSIS investigators, I learned that the IRA investigation was one of the few actual terrorism investigations carried out during the period of transition, when the RCMP Security Service was disbanded to make room for the new civilian CSIS. An interlocutor informed me that there was little concern that Irish extremists would plan and carry out a terrorist attack in Canada, but rather that they would raise funds for the cause in Ireland. Interestingly,

I also found out that there were instances in which IRA sympathisers would steal—or "procure"—blasting caps and detonators from various places in Canada, especially Northern Ontario mining sites, and send them to the group back home.

While I am unaware of any court cases that prosecuted IRA sympathisers in this regard, there was an instance in the US in the early 1990s. Six men (including one "resident alien" in Toronto) were tried but acquitted on charges of acquiring 2,900 detonators from a mine in Arizona. The judge found that the government's case had collected evidence that was circumstantial: the lawyer of one of the defendants stated, "It's clear the government went to excess based on some stereotype of the Irish community and Irish culture."[14]

Why was this activity so prevalent? For several reasons. This equipment is legal and can be obtained legitimately. Additionally, it is used in mining and detonation operations, such as for road clearance. Northern Ontario is well known for mining operations and it is likely that blasting caps are ubiquitous. It would be next to impossible to maintain a foolproof inventory of each one and its location.

The IRA could use these blasting caps to construct improvised explosive devices (IEDs), which indeed it did in the perpetration of many terrorist attacks in Ireland and England. Some of those attacks may have been aided by equipment manufactured in Canada.

I do not know when the IRA investigations ceased in Canada—they were certainly no longer active to the best of my knowledge when I joined CSIS in 2001. While it never appeared to be a priority for either the RCMP or CSIS, it was nevertheless a requirement for these two agencies to do their due diligence since Canada could not be seen as a haven for terrorists or an easy place to operate in the furtherance of attacks abroad.

A month after 9/11 the Canadian daily, the *Globe and Mail*, reported that, according to "intelligence sources," "as many as ten members of the deadly Irish Republican Army slipped into Canada over the summer to raise money to support their terror campaign back home."[15] In light of the shifted focus of Canadian border officials to interdict "suspected terrorists of Middle Eastern descent," alleged IRA terrorists were getting a "free pass." Those same sources reported that "the IRA has traditionally seen Canada as a rich and reliable source of money to finance its propaganda campaigns and weapons purchases abroad." This is undoubtedly true.

Lastly, while the IRA and its offspring appear to pose less of a threat today than they did decades ago, it is important to bear in mind that the cause for which they fought—that is, a united Ireland and the ouster of the UK from the north—is yet to be achieved. The implication of this is that the IRA or a similar group could undertake violent actions to meet this goal.

We have a tendency to conclude that grievances have shelf lives. Once a group is defeated or its membership fades away we resign them to the ash heap of history. Sometimes the grievances are resolved to the satisfaction of those willing to engage in violence to accomplish their mission. The African National Congress is a good example: it was certainly seen as a terrorist outfit by some but transformed into a purely political party when Apartheid in South Africa ended in the 1990s.

Not all terrorists go quietly. The Irish problem has been with us for centuries, and violent extremist groups for more than 150 years, as long as Canada has been an independent nation. If certain parties conclude that an adequate solution to this issue is not forthcoming, it is possible, if not probable, that some will resort to violence. Canada was once home to sympathisers willing to support violence. It is not inconceivable that CSIS, the RCMP, and their partners may one day have to relaunch investigations on this terrorist threat.

Getting back to T. D. McGee, a great Canadian was felled by a terrorist metres away from the very seat of democratic government terrorists hate and seek to upend. We will see more such instances in the acts to come.

French Canadian Terrorism

The province of Quebec has held two referendums (or, as some used to call them in English Canada, "neverendums") to seek the support of the provincial population to leave Canada. It was not called "separation" *per se* but rather "sovereignty-association," an arrangement some compared to "divorce with bedroom privileges." As this is a book on terrorism, and not political science, I will not delve into the details of what this meant.

As it turned out, I had a front row seat at both votes, the first in May 1980 and the second in October 1995. During the former I was an exchange student in a Quebec government work placement centre and had just arrived in the provincial capital from my home in London, Ontario. My first day of work was the morning after the vote: the no side (those who wanted to remain in Canada) had handily won by a margin of almost 60 percent to 40 percent for the "splitters." I entered my new office with trepidation as an anglophone from a very anglophone city in a majority anglophone province. My French was good but not great, as the whole point of the exchange was to learn to speak French better.

I did not know what to expect from my new colleagues. Would I be rejected as an English Canadian? Would I face hostility? None of that came to pass. The civil servants talked about the results for a few minutes over coffee and then went back to their jobs. It almost came across as a non-event.

The second referendum in October 1995 was very different both in terms of the result and of my role during it. A late surge in nationalist support gave impetus to the yes side so that when the ballots were tallied, separation was only narrowly defeated. I mean very narrowly: 50.58 percent to 49.42 percent. We came that close to breaking up as a country.

When the vote took place, I was a multilingual analyst at CSE. I was also a senior analyst and was among those with experience asked to stay overnight to monitor foreign reaction to whatever would come out of the vote. This was in keeping with CSE's foreign intelligence mandate.

As I and my colleagues gathered around for the broadcast of the results, I will never forget a very emotional Jacques Parizeau, head of the Parti Québecois (PQ), claim that Quebecers had come so close to their destiny, only to have been defeated by "money and the ethnic vote". We were all shocked at this overtly racist statement.

So, what about the foreign reaction? If memory serves me well the whole affair was met with a collective yawn around the world and by 1 a.m. we were pretty well done our tasks, although I do recall staying awake (barely!) until 7 a.m. that morning. Would countries have acted differently if the yes camp had won? Perhaps. I guess we will never know.

Since 1995 Quebec has eschewed a third kick at the referendum can. Support for separation or sovereignty association has never risen significantly over the past twenty-five years and I would wager that most Canadians feel that this threat to our nation is ancient history. "Never say never" as the adage goes, but the fact remains that we have not been subjected to another vote.

It is important to underscore that these efforts to use French Canadian nationalism to gain a new relationship with the rest of Canada were peaceful in nature. As already suggested above, we in Canada like to remind our friends abroad that while the US had to fight a bloody revolution against Great Britain to become independent, we and England did so non-violently, through an act of the British Parliament (the British North America Act of 1867). Quebec followed this historical tradition, using ballots and not bullets to determine its fate.

It was not always so.

In the 1960s and very early 1970s Quebec was rocked by terrorist attacks that took several lives, damaged public property, and led to the imposition of the War Measures Act in 1970. We are referring here to the violent methods deployed by the Front de libération du Québec (FLQ) ("Quebec Liberation Front") primarily in Montreal.

Rather than discuss the origins of this terrorist group, I refer the reader to other more comprehensive histories of the FLQ, for example, D'Arcy Jenish's The *Making of the October Crisis: Canada's long nightmare of terrorism at the hands of the FLQ*. Here the focus will be on the acts perpetrated by the group, the atmosphere of fear in the province, and the ultimate decision to declare martial law in the wake of two kidnappings in October 1970, as well as the impressions of those in the RCMP, including the Security Service, who investigated these violent extremists.

The FLQ began its campaign of violence in 1963 and at first limited its placement of crude bombs to mailboxes and armouries, especially in the Westmount area of Montreal, a wealthy English suburb. This strategy of course made sense as the FLQ wanted to rid the province of Anglophone influence. The group also engaged in bank holdups and one hostage-taking which led to a draconian crackdown in October 1970 by the Trudeau government (led by Pierre Elliott Trudeau, the current prime minister's father).

From 1963 to 1970 the group engaged in at least 160 violent actions which led to the deaths of several people and the injuries of many more. For example, twenty-seven people were wounded when an FLQ bomb went off at the Montreal Stock Exchange on February 13, 1969.

The most famous terrorist attack for which the FLQ was responsible was without question the kidnapping of UK Trade Commissioner James Cross on October 5, 1970, and that of Quebec Labour Minister and Vice Premier, Pierre Laporte, five days later. This led to what is referred to in Canada as the October Crisis and the imposition of martial law by the

Trudeau Liberal government. The invocation of the War Measures Act was the first such move by any Canadian government in peacetime. A total of 453 people believed to have ties to the FLQ were arrested: 435 were released without charge.

James Cross was released by the FLQ on December 3, 1970, in a deal whereby the terrorists were granted safe passage to Cuba. Pierre Laporte was killed by his captors shortly after he had been seized. His body was discovered in the trunk of a car belonging to Paul Rose, an FLQ leader, on October 17, 1970.

I was fortunate to speak with a retired RCMP officer who worked for the Security Service as of 1966. The details below are all derived from our conversation. He worked in what was known as Section D-1, separatism and counterterrorism (Section D was responsible for counter-subversion). Some would balk at the juxtaposition of these two terms, bristling at the suggestion that all those who sought independence for Quebec were necessarily terrorists. Yet, in light of the bombing campaign in Montreal, was it really that much of a stretch to consider at least the violent separatist fringe terrorists?

By 1968 the RCMP Security Service effort against violent extremists was still small, at least in Montreal: twelve or so officers. The unit was paired with the Montreal municipal police force in what was termed the Combined Anti-Terrorist Squad (CATS). One of the priorities was to carry out background checks on members of the RIN (Rassemblement pour l'indépendence nationale or Rally for National Independance) who were seeking security clearances. In those days having separatist leanings precluded one from receiving a security clearance.

Of course, by that time a whole series of bombs had gone off. The atmosphere was frantic: my contact noted that CATS had to investigate somewhere in the neighbourhood of 168 bombings (real or called in) over the course of a year. There was also a need to look into armed robberies that the violent extremists carried out to support their activities. Raids were carried out, and bombs and guns were discovered.

The pace of investigations was so high that there was no time to worry about policy. Sources had to be recruited and paid: my contact noted that one particular agent, who was related to a member of the cell that kidnapped James Cross, was paid $15 a week (the agent thought this pay was "wonderful"). That one source was among the best recruited and played an instrumental role in the location of Mr. Cross.

My Security Service contact noted that prior to the Cross kidnapping the FLQ had attempted to carry out two other similar operations: that of the Israeli and US ambassadors. The RCMP and Montreal Police foiled both plots and discovered leaflets the kidnappers were planning to distribute had they successfully seized the American diplomat.

According to my contact, the ethos of the members of CATS at the time was that they were involved in criminal, not terrorism, operations. As he noted, "We carried a gun everyday as a police officer." The mentality was that of law enforcement.

When James Cross was seized on October 5 the squad began to receive hundreds of tips ("the public went crazy"). They all had to be taken seriously and run to ground. It seemed as if everyone had seen someone that looked like Cross. Most of these tips turned out to be false. My contact wanted to develop his own agent, who had been providing good insights and actionable intelligence on the FLQ and did so together with a sergeant who worked in counter-espionage.

After Cross was found alive, attention turned to those who killed Laporte. The Sûreté du Québec had been unable to locate the assassins but with the RCMP's assistance finally did so—a sniffer dog located Paul Rose and his accomplices hiding in a hole under the furnace in the basement in a farmhouse! Much of the success came thanks to incredibly intense surveillance. One finding would lead to another, which would lead to another, and so on.

My Security Service contact claims that the FLQ put out a "contract" on him for his role in wrapping up the movement, as after the October Crisis the FLQ was only ever a shadow of its former self and never engaged in violence again. Intercepted communications had demonstrated that several individuals were willing to put up money for the Security Service member's head.

What I found very interesting in talking to those who worked in the RCMP Security Service was that the investigations carried out on the FLQ were covered by the Force's "subversion" focus, not terrorism. There are probably a few good reasons for this, and the primary one may be that Canada did not recognise terrorism as a criminal offence until after 9/11. You cannot investigate an individual or group with the intention of laying criminal charges when there are no charges that cover terrorism.

Secondly, as seen through the eyes of the Canadian government at the time, the FLQ was trying to subvert the essence of state authority. Interestingly, the CSIS Act still makes an oblique reference to subversion in section 2, which defines the threats it is authorised to investigate as follows: "activities directed toward undermining by covert unlawful acts or directed toward or intended ultimately to lead to the destruction or overthrow by violence of, the constitutionally established system of government in Canada."

After the October Crisis, violent Quebec nationalism subsided. No more would kidnappings, bombs or bank robberies be part of the quest for Quebec independence. Was the average Quebecois disgusted with the methods used by the FLQ? Or was separatism just not a priority with the majority? Whatever the answer, Canadians were no longer faced with an existential threat to national unity that sought to use violence to intimidate us.

I will leave the last word on this to two people. First, D'Arcy Jenish, the author of the single best book on the topic, who on the occasion of the 50th anniversary of the October Crisis and in the midst of a demand by some that the current Trudeau government issue an apology for the declaration of the War Measures Act, wrote in a *Globe and Mail* article:

> Felquistes, as these terrorists became known, stole hundreds of pounds of dynamite from quarries and construction sites. They were responsible for more than 200 bombings. They committed dozens of armed robberies and caused the deaths of six people, including a 16-year-old who was planting a bomb and a 65-year-old night watchman who was about to retire. All this before the kidnappings and before Mr. Laporte was murdered by two of the four men who abducted him at gunpoint, on the Saturday evening of Thanksgiving weekend, while he played catch with his nephew in front of his suburban home. By any reasonable definition, it was the radical and misguided young hotheads of the FLQ who were guilty of "extreme violence," not the Government of Canada.[16]

In response to a blog post on my website in which I commented on that same anniversary, I received this response from a longstanding security professional in Canada:

> As a high school teenager of French descent and resident in Montreal—to this day I will never forget the sound of solemn music on all radio stations the evening of October 17, 1970 and owed to the discovery of Deputy Premier Pierre Laporte's body in the trunk of a car after having been kidnapped by the FLQ "Chenier

Cell" a week earlier. Québecers—both French and English—were gripped in fear, not only of the kidnappings of Laporte and James Cross, but also owing to the many bombings since the early 1960s. Those terrorist actions far overstepped the customary culture of our citizenry which was accustomed to political process, debate, and negotiation—rather than violence. It seemed to me that my family, friends, and most citizens condemned the violence—that had killed several and injured many; and we were grateful to have the protection of Police and Military at the time. The threat was quelled, martial law quickly lifted and peace restored. The War Measures Act may not have been perfectly expedited—but it certainly was not allowed to remain and fester to the significant detriment of democracy.

Still, as the 50th anniversary of the October Crisis drew near in 2020, I began to see more op-ed pieces in leading Canadian dailies penned by those with no apparent experience in counterterrorism, demanding that the Trudeau government (led by Justin Trudeau, Pierre Trudeau's son) apologise to all Quebecers for the imposition of martial law during that time. Saying sorry for rounding up terrorists? How Canadian.

Paul Rose's son, Felix, has made a documentary film about his family which has been labelled by some as an attempt to lionise a terrorist and whitewash history, turning murderers into heroes. According to a "cultural commentator," some Quebec nationalists appear to be drawn by the film's "romantic portrayal of the militants" and may be eager to revive historical grievances, thereby giving their waning cause a "spark."[17]

Not surprisingly, I find these calls for an apology ridiculous. Canada's security agencies did what they had to in order to put an end to a terrorism campaign that had lasted the better part of a decade. People had been killed; others maimed. A small group of violent extremists were trying to use terrorism to force political change. Undoubtedly, mistakes were made in the course of the government's response, but no Canadian official has any need to say sorry for defeating a terrorist movement.

None.

Terrorism at the Montreal Olympics?

To Canadians, the 1976 Olympic Summer Games elicit both great pride and a little bit of embarrassment. We were very happy that Canada was going to host the Games for the first time (we have since been the venue for the Winter Games in Calgary (1988) and Vancouver (2010)). On the embarrassing side we became the only country to host the games from which not a single gold medal was won. The construction of the site was rife with corruption, and the hallmark of the site, the Olympic Stadium, was immediately nicknamed "the big O." In light of the massive cost overruns that was quickly changed to "the big Owe."

While the games went off without a hitch, at least from the security side, this should not be interpreted as illustrating that nothing was happening in the background. My RCMP Security Service contact told me that there was concern that a repeat of the 1972 Munich Olympics massacre would occur. In this light, then, there were efforts afoot to ensure that no Middle East terrorist group would target the Israeli athletes, or any others for that matter.

One threat that came to the attention of the Security Service at the time originated in what many would see as an unlikely corner: Jewish extremism. It was learned that the Jewish Defense League (JDL) and one of its co-founders were looking into conducting an attack at the Games to, in the words of my contact, "attempt retribution." Intelligence gained through a highly placed human source indicated that the JDL had developed poison pens (real poison pens, not metaphorical ones!) to be used in assassinations. Nothing of the sort occurred in Montreal in 1976. Nevertheless, it was a good reminder that extremism in Canada comes from all sides.

As an aside, there were also terrorism concerns in the lead up to Expo 67, the international fair in Montreal. Any time an event of this scale is held there is always preparation put in place to ensure that nothing goes awry. In the end nothing amiss occurred.

Armenian Terrorism

One of the longest standing disagreements over a historical grievance that has led to terrorist attacks around the world is the 1915 Armenian genocide. As World War I raged, and the Ottoman Empire, the "sick man of Europe", was in its dying days, the government in Istanbul engaged in the expulsion of millions of Armenian nationals who it believed were fifth columnists, or in the very least were unwanted.

Estimates of those who died during this expulsion vary widely. At the upper end it is believed that more than a million and a half people were killed outright in massacres or in the forced marches to the Syrian desert. Turkey has countered that the death toll was much smaller and that there was never any orchestrated genocide.

Not surprisingly a few groups have turned to violence to draw attention to the genocide and gain a degree of retribution. Among the modern groups are:

- the Armenian Secret Army for the Liberation of Armenia (ASALA)
- the Armenian Liberation Front
- the Justice Commandos for the Armenian Genocide (JCAG)
- the Armenian Liberation Movement
- the Armenian Revolutionary Army (ARA)

As we shall see, both ASALA (described to me by one contact as "Marxist" in outlook) and the ARA carried out attacks in Canada in the 1980s.

But first a personal story.

In August 1982 I was heading back to my hometown from Ottawa to begin a master's degree at UWO. I had been in Ottawa over the summer working as a translator-in-training at the Multilingual Services Bureau of Canada's Secretary of State. My tasks included translating Spanish documents into English for Canadian government clients. It afforded a wonderful insight into this line of work—one I would be fortunate enough to enjoy when I joined CSE less than a year later, albeit for work of a very different nature!

As I was heading west along what is known as "the 417," that portion of the Trans-Canada Highway that passes through Ottawa, I came across a police roadblock. Some RCMP officers carrying some pretty scary firearms were stopping all cars, asking some questions and taking a look inside. I was quickly allowed to continue. I had no idea what this was all about.

It turned out that on that very morning, August 27, 1982, the Turkish Military Attaché to Canada, Atilla Altikat, was killed while sitting in his car at a stoplight along the Sir John A. Macdonald Parkway (a scenic road along the Ottawa River) at Island Park Drive. A car had pulled up and a gunman fired several shots into the attaché, killing him instantly, before running into a nearby grove of trees. No suspect was ever found.[18] Both ASALA and the Justice Commandos issued statements claiming the attack. It was the first—and to the best of my memory the only—killing of a foreign diplomat in Canadian history. One contact confided to me that there was intelligence (i.e., SIGINT) that an attack was coming and that there were ties to Armenian extremists in the US (which would necessitate bilateral cooperation).

This act of terrorism was probably the reason why an investigation into Armenian extremism was one of the few active counterterrorism investigations on the go when CSIS was created. And this killing was not the only one. But first, back to my personal story.

Scarcely two and a half years later I was at CSE, working as a multilingual analyst, already developing what would turn into a two-decade specialisation on the Middle East. Still, we were not looking at Armenian terrorism, despite obvious connections to that part of the world. In fact, we were not looking at terrorism at all.

On March 12, 1985, news came in that there was a hostage-taking at the Turkish Embassy in Ottawa's tony Sandy Hill district, home to many embassies, high commissions and consulates. Again, SIGINT had given some early warning of a possible attack. A part-time security guard, Claude Brunette, also a 31-year-old University of Ottawa student, confronted a group of three men who had scaled the embassy's security perimeter and fired shots at the security hut. Mr. Brunette was hit by two shots which killed him instantly, although he got a few shots away at the intruders.

The trio proceeded to blow open the main door, enter the embassy and take upwards of a dozen hostages. The Ambassador, Coskun Kirca, escaped when he jumped from a second-floor window, breaking several bones. The crisis ended several hours later when the terrorists, who claimed to be from the ARA, surrendered: no hostages were harmed.

The three claimed that they had taken their action to "make Turkey pay" for the 1915 genocide. All three were tried, convicted, and sentenced to life in prison.[19] They were all released in 2010 ("life" rarely means life in the Canadian justice system).

Largely in response to these two attacks Canadian security services' monitoring of Armenian extremism in Canada continued until the end of the 1980s. One contact told me that the tradecraft used by Armenian extremists who were on the radar was quite good, in contrast with many Islamist terrorists we will examine in the next chapter. They were described as professional, knowing exactly what they wanted to achieve—a Turkish apology and independence for Armenia) —and would do anything to meet their goals. By 1990 there was still high-level concern that more attacks were pending.

Then, it abruptly stopped. As one of my contacts who worked on that task told me, the threat seemed to dissipate. This was a fortunate occurrence as the team looking at the Armenian issue was small. In my contact's reckoning, the dissolution of the Soviet Union and Armenia's subsequent independence took some wind out of the terrorists' sails. The new nation had to face a new cause célèbre in the so-called Nagorno-Karabakh conflict with neighbouring fellow new nation, Azerbaijan. That never-ending dispute has led to its own terrorism over the decades. Interestingly, as this book was being drafted, renewed clashes broke out between the two nations in July 2020,[20] demonstrating that nationalist causes such as these can have very long lifespans. We will return to this at the end of this chapter.

Something else occurred during the height of the Armenian investigations that puts security intelligence work in a different light. One of my contacts who was responsible for such tasks confided to me that when his efforts to interview members of the community to recruit sources became more widely known it was conveyed to him that there were rumours that some extremists in that milieu wanted to have him killed for his attempts to penetrate this world.

I do not imagine threats of this nature are any different than those faced by law enforcement officers who are looking into organised crime or street gang networks. These actors do not want to have their activities thwarted and do not take kindly to any attempt to infiltrate their closed societies with the intent to gather intelligence or evidence that would lead to action which would interfere with their programs.

I am not aware of any other specific instance of a real danger of violence to an officer who was "just doing their job." This all points to the fact that those who work in security intelligence or law enforcement toil in a dangerous world. Terrorists and other criminals live for violence after all. In particular, terrorists are driven by a sense of purpose, based on some perverted ideological goal, and often see their mission as inspired, hence their anger at having a local agency doing what it can to interfere with their plans. Terrorism is indeed a nasty business.

Even if the watchful eye on Armenian terrorists ended, the grievance that led to the alphabet's soup of extremist groups did not. Ottoman Turkey is still accused of carrying out a genocide against its Armenian population. The modern Turkish state has never admitted responsibility for the massacre; and, with uber nationalist Recep Tayyip Erdogan as Turkish president, it is highly unlikely to do so. If there are any groups still seeking to punish Turkey, their rationale is still valid.

As one contact told me, this form of violent extremism may see a generational turnover. The Nagorno-Karabakh issue may be the match that kindles the fire for the new generation.

Anti-Cuban Terrorism

In the wake of the takeover of Cuba by the Communist-led band headed by Fidel Castro, the Caribbean island all of a sudden became a worrying threat a few hundred kilometres off the south coast of the US. In hindsight this all looks like an overblown assessment of the danger Cuba posed to the US, and by extension the West. Still, the 1962 Cuban missile crisis—plans by the Soviet Union to station ballistic missiles on the island—did bring the world as close to World War III as we may have ever been.

Many Cubans fled to the US and took up campaigns to undermine the Castro regime. We have all read of the US Central Intelligence Agency (CIA) plots to kill Castro—the use of exploding cigars is my personal favourite. There are other sources the reader can access to explore this period.

There were a handful of acts which could very well be called terrorism that were committed in our country by what must have been anti-Castro elements. Here is a list (believed to be comprehensive) from the website of the Canadian Network on Cuba:[21]

- 1966 – A bazooka attack took place against the Cuban Embassy in Ottawa and bombs exploded at the Cuban trade offices in Ottawa.
- 1967 – An explosive device was detonated at the Cuba Pavilion at Expo in Montreal; a bomb exploded at the warehouses of Fraser Brothers, a Canadian firm trading with Cuba; and Cuban trade offices were bombed in Montreal.
- 1969 – A bomb was placed in the doorway of the Cuban Consulate in Montreal but failed to go off.
- 1972 – A bomb exploded at the Cuban Consulate in Montreal, killing an official named Sergio Perez Castillo.
- 1974 – A bomb exploded in the Cuban Embassy in Ottawa.
- 1976 – An explosive device was lobbed at the Cuban Consulate in Montreal.
- 1980 – A bomb was set off at the Cuban Consulate in Montreal.
- 1980 – A bomb was set off at the Cuban Consulate in Montreal.

This era in Canada seems largely forgotten by most Canadians. I did not find any additional sources to provide further insight into these attacks.

Sikh Terrorism

We live in a post 9/11 world where the events of that Tuesday in September in New York and Washington have defined for most of us what terrorism is and where it is coming from. The deaths of almost 3,000 people in a single act of violent extremism is without precedent in the history of the world: one hopes it will never be superseded. The perpetrators of that act, Islamist terrorists, have also provided us with the paradigm of modern terrorism. It is not surprising that the largest single chapter of this book will look in some detail at the Islamist terrorist threat to Canada.

And yet it was not always so, especially here in the "great white north." Prior to the deliberate flying of airplanes into buildings, the largest previous terrorist attack had nothing to do with jihad. It was tied to Sikh terrorism. And it had its genesis in Canada.

On June 23, 1985, Air India Flight 182, which had originated in Vancouver, was bombed out of the sky off the coast of Ireland, killing all 329 people aboard (307 passengers and 22 crew). Before 9/11 it was the single greatest terrorist attack—at least on a civilian airliner—in history.

The bomb had been placed on the aircraft by Canadian Sikh terrorists. The history of Sikh terrorism is a long one, and not only in Canada. Many countries, including India itself where the grievances that Sikh extremists claim had their birth, have suffered from violence in the furtherance of the Sikh cause.

In a nutshell, the desire for an independent Sikh homeland within India, named "Khalistan," and the Indian government's refusal to consider such, is at the centre of Sikh terrorism. More narrowly, the Indian army's decision, right or wrong, to lay siege to the Golden Temple in Amritsar in June 1984 (called Operation Bluestar) to oust a fanatic fringe which had taken control, was akin to waving a red flag in front of a bull. The site is sacred to the minority Sikhs and the army's invasion was seen as sacrilege. The assassination of Indian Prime Minister Indira Gandhi by two of her Sikh bodyguards in October of that same year was definitively tied to that decision. And so was the Air India bombing.

In the wake of the terrorist attack, and the collective failure to prevent it, the Canadian government launched an inquiry, the Commission of Inquiry into the Investigation of the Bombing of Air India Flight 182, chaired by retired Supreme Court of Canada Judge, John Major. The inquiry did not begin until June 2006, twenty-two years after the tragedy (how Canadian!) and concluded four years later. The result was a multi-volume report.

I will not review or summarise the contents of this report—the conclusions and recommendations of the inquiry are part of the public record.

What I can do, which I think is of relevance and may not be well known in the public domain, is to reflect on the sentiment at the time with respect to Sikh terrorism, and more specifically the Air India attack, from the perspective of someone who worked within the Canadian intelligence community, as I was a multilingual analyst at CSE during that period. Furthermore, many of the former CSIS and RCMP agents I spoke with were also on duty at that time.

I recall that those of us at CSE were seized with the events inside India at the time of the Golden Temple affair. We came across information that provided us with interesting perspectives on what was happening: for obvious reasons I cannot go into more detail on the nature of that information.

Suffice to say that we were supplying the Canadian government with real-time intelligence on what was transpiring in India. There was ample information on developments: not complete perhaps, as intelligence is rarely, if ever, complete, but very good raw intelligence that the Canadian government could use in its own assessment of what was happening.

The other aspect of this tragedy is the reality that CSIS was not even a year old when Air India Flight 182 was bombed. I state that as a fact, not an excuse. As already noted, CSIS saw the light of day in July of 1984 when it was decided to create a civilian security service out of the RCMP Security Service. The new agency, staffed in large part by former RCMP officers, was still finding its bearings.

Having said that, many former CSIS agents confided to me that, yes, Sikh terrorism was a priority in 1984, insofar as counterterrorism was a priority at the time. Allow me to explain.

Recall that CSIS has four investigative priorities: the activities of foreign intelligence agencies in Canada, foreign interference, terrorism, and subversion. In 1984 terrorism simply did not have the limelight it does now. CI ruled the roost.

CI investigations are very different than CT ones on several levels. The end game in CI is not to gather evidence to proceed to prosecution in a Canadian court. The goal is to amass enough information (i.e., intelligence) to demonstrate that a given individual (or individuals) on a posting to Canada from a foreign state, whether as an officially recognised diplomat or not, is engaged in activities "not consistent with the duties of a foreign representative." In other words, spying. Once that determination is made the next step is to deport that person. No charges. No court case. No disclosure of sensitive information in a public hearing. Just a formal letter to the embassy in question that so-and-so no longer has the protection of international treaties and is no longer welcome in Canada. Bye-bye former spy. Unless of course the organisation could "turn" the spy and get them to work for you and report on other spies.

In CT investigations there is no question of declaring someone persona non grata. The goal is to gather evidence to lay charges under the Canadian Criminal Code (section 83.01 ff) and bring the case to court. This has all kinds of implications for intelligence to evidence which will be discussed in the penultimate chapter. The acts alleged to be in the planning stages are criminal offences in Canada. The end game is to investigate these individuals and arrest them before the bomb goes off, not after.

One contact, a former CSIS agent, told me that early classes of intelligence officers spent a great deal of time on CI tradecraft (i.e., how spies operate abroad) and very little on CT matters. To those early employees, terrorism was a phenomenon which would eventually end up as a crime (that of planning to kill people) and would hence be best handled by the police.

Resources were always a challenge since they are not infinite. As CI was seen as the priority it ruled the roost. It got first dibs on things such as "spin teams" (i.e., physical surveillance). CT was a poor country cousin in this regard.

In 1984, with the exception of the cases discussed in this chapter (Sikh and Armenian extremism primarily) there was no CT to speak of. One former CSIS agent (who was ex-RCMP) confided to me that there was very little CT experience and knowledge in the Service in 1984. All the best minds were devoted to CI, despite the fact that investigations of these cases were a "slow burn" that took years of investigative legwork to get anywhere. CSIS was also still trying to find its feet when it had to look at the Sikh terrorism issue so soon after its creation There was also the added complication that relations with the RCMP, where some members still resented the fact that a new civilian spy agency had been carved out of the Force, were not the best.

Nevertheless, with respect to Sikh terrorism there was an effort to carry out investigations in Canada. It did become the counterterrorism priority for CSIS after Air India. In addition to the lack of CT experience, however, there were some obstacles in carrying out this task. The Sikh issue was described to me as a "steep learning curve." CSIS had to do a quick study not only on what was happening in Canada but also on what was happening back in India since, as already noted, events overseas had a huge impact on the development of Sikh terrorism here. It was described to me as a period of turmoil.

Canadian security agencies were able to infiltrate a few human sources into the extremist milieu in Canada and were able to get a partial picture post-Air India on who could pose a possible future threat. But as one contact told me, having a few sources does not give you a comprehensive overview of the community.

Interestingly, a related event arose in 1987 that complicated matters for CSIS agents. The organisation's first (and up to that time, only) director, Thomas D'Arcy ("Ted") Finn, was forced to resign over allegations that CSIS had used information from an "unreliable human source" to obtain a Federal Court intercept warrant in a case involving the shooting of an Indian cabinet minister in British Columbia (see below). The loss of the director sidelined many in CSIS at the time as it became necessary to review all court warrants to ensure that other warrants were not equally problematic. One contact confided to me that morale was negatively affected.

With respect to getting local citizens in the Sikh community on side, buy-in turned out to be difficult. Developing a relationship with specific individuals and local leaders is critical for a security intelligence service. Aside from the bread-and-butter issue of human source recruitment, security services need to convey their concerns to a broader audience. Once other members of a given community are made aware of such concerns they can act as a force multiplier on information gathering. These people do not have to act as paid human sources per se but usually have information that is critical to the Service's understanding of the threat environment.

This proved to be hard to achieve in the first half of the 1980s in Canada. Gurdwaras (Sikh temples) were often at a minimum wary of CSIS and law enforcement or at a maximum fully aware of and supportive of violent Sikh elements in their midst. Operation Blue Star had kindled a flame of anger and desire for retribution in Canada and there were those willing, if not keen, to fan it. Nevertheless, with time the relationship between CSIS/law enforcement and Sikh leaders got better. The latter was led to understand why CSIS was interested, particularly in the activities of terrorist groups such as the Babbar Khalsa, the International Sikh Youth Federation (ISYF) and the World Sikh Organisation (WSO).

CSIS collection efforts were also hampered by the fact that while most people in these communities did not outwardly support the use of violence, there was a reluctance to inform on those who did. Many communities were split on the issue of the quest for independence, and violence within gurdwaras was common as the two sides fought for influence. Some of these institutions were taken over for all intents by Sikh extremists. As one former CSIS agent told me, "the Serbs and Croats had nothing on the Sikhs!" As a side note, growing up in London, Ontario, in the 1960s and 1970s, everyone knew that the last place you wanted to be was at the local soccer pitch when the Serbs and Croats faced off against one another: knife fights were a regular feature in the crowds at these matches!

Eventually, CSIS went from being a social pariah to achieving some level of success in its intelligence collection and community outreach efforts. It began to identify who the problem players were and was able to initiate investigations on them, including some of the actors responsible for the Air India bombing. It was also determined that fundraising for activities was an issue.

Still, there was a perception that the government of the day was not overly concerned about Sikh terrorism in Canada or about the Sikh issue itself. It was simply not a priority. Recall that intelligence services take their marching orders from elected officials and senior public servants. In my days at CSE, I regularly took part in the annual foreign intelligence requirements process, wherein intelligence requirements were developed by a bevy of government departments, and it was those requirements that drove CSE's collection and reporting. CSIS did not perceive that intelligence requirements on the Sikh situation were forthcoming, or that they were forthcoming strongly enough, from the Conservative government in 1984.

Investigations were further complicated by the high levels of immigration from Sikh-populated areas of India, though this is not to be construed as a criticism of immigration policies in Canada. The influx of potentially large numbers of Sikh extremists fleeing a precarious situation in India before and after the Golden Temple siege made the work of CSIS (and other agencies such as Immigration and Border Services) that much harder.

This speaks to a larger issue in Canada that requires further commentary. Canada is a nation of immigrants and has been since the 16th century, much to the detriment of its First Nations. What was initially a French, then British-French, nation has blossomed into a multilingual and multicultural land. In recent years Canada has welcomed as much as 1 percent of our current population (38.7 million as of 2023) each year. These new Canadians have made outstanding contributions to who we are.

And yet it would be extremely naïve to ignore that a small number of these immigrants have brought homeland issues and grievances with them. As a matter of fact, almost all the acts of terrorism discussed in this book, ranging from T. D. McGee's assassination to the jihadi plots to be discussed in the next chapter, are tied to conflicts outside of Canada. The Sikh terrorist problem is no different. It stands to reason, then, that some of those who emigrated to Canada from India in the early 1980s could have contributed to the existence of Sikh violent extremism in this country.

One contact told me that at the time of the Air India bombing there were simply too many targets to keep an eye on. This is is the CSIS term used to describe someone who is the subject of a security investigation: it has a very different meaning in a military context. A young organisation with a young cadre of intelligence officers engaged in a steep learning curve simply could not keep pace with the number of individuals who needed to be watched to determine capability and intent. As a result, the intelligence required to prevent acts like those of Air India Flight 182 was found wanting.

There was another factor that may have hampered CSIS's ability to investigate Sikh terrorism in Canada. Recall that in the early 1980s CSE was producing good SIGINT reporting on Sikh terrorism in India and that country's response to it. As a matter of course, CSE provided its intelligence reports to Government of Canada customers. CSIS was one of those customers, as was the RCMP.

The problem was that SIGINT reports were not being read regularly at CSIS and as a result the intelligence contained therein was not available to help in that organisation's investigations. There were several reasons for this. First and foremost, SIGINT is the highest classified intelligence produced in Canada, at Top Secret or higher. The perceived sensitivity of this type of intelligence led to its restricted distribution within CSIS. To view it, an agent had to go to a special office and read it on site. We all know what happens when something is made hard to use: we do not use it.

In addition, the nature of SIGINT made the use of it in investigations difficult. Whether it was the source of the intelligence or its method of collection, it was seen as complicated.Intelligence officers saw this as an unnecessary burden added to their work. The situation at the RCMP was worse. As one contact told me, "The Mounties always have that little black book with them!" This is a reference to the information to be used as evidence in a criminal case that could go to court, and hence be disclosed in public. One thing is certain among SIGINT agencies: they do not want their information made public!

It is impossible to say whether the non-use of SIGINT made that much of a difference. Nevertheless, in a security investigation you want all the intelligence available to help you understand what you have and to help point you in the right direction to obtain what you do not. SIGINT could certainly have helped in that regard. In the end, a decision was made to place CSE customer relations officers (CROs) at CSIS HQ to facilitate the use of this crucial form of intelligence.

One further elephant in the room, while highly condemnatory, needs to be mentioned. As one contact who worked Sikh terrorism at CSIS in the mid-1980s confided to me, a huge factor in the failure to prevent Air India from occurring was the hatred and animosity felt by the RCMP toward the nascent CSIS. Besides those in the RCMP who resented the creation of CSIS and the closure of the Security Service, some felt that "terrorism is a crime" and as a result should be investigated by the police, not a bunch of civilian university graduates with no experience in the field. It is difficult for me to judge how much influence this dismissal had in what was missed.

A contact did confide to me that the security intelligence community was well aware that there were individuals committed to carrying out violence in Canada or abroad in the furtherance of Sikh independence. Many very good investigations were carried out and a great deal was learned.

But not enough, soon enough.

In the end, however, the inability of CSIS, the RCMP, and their partners to stop the bombing of that aircraft and the subsequent loss of hundreds of lives must be called what it is: a failure, and a catastrophic one at that. Those of us who worked in this world of security intelligence all know that we are collectively at risk of getting it wrong. We accept that we are only perceived as competent up to our last failure. As I mentioned earlier, few know or care when we get it right and foil planned terrorist plots, but everyone is quick to point fingers and assign blame when we mess up.

This is not a bitter complaint but rather a recognition of reality. Bad news always gets more coverage than good: ask any journalist. Efforts that go into arresting wannabe terrorists on the eve of executing their acts of mayhem are usually treated with a public shrug But get it wrong once and there is hell to pay. In an analogous way, the IRA had it right when it said in the wake of the failed Brighton bombing in 1984 targeting UK Prime Minister Margaret Thatcher, "Today, we were unlucky. But remember, we only have to be lucky once—you have to be lucky always." There is obviously much more than luck in successful CT investigations, but it is also true that 100 percent success is the only expectation.

In the wake of the Air India terrorist attack the investigation into Sikh terrorism only increased. As one of my contacts expressed it, the Canadian Solicitor General made it known that resources would be provided to carry out CT operations: many intelligence officers (IOs) were told to move from CI investigations to CT ones. Public safety (i.e., CT) trumped all else as a priority for CSIS work and no one balked at this. How could they after more than 300 people had been killed in a cowardly act of terrorism? The individual described this time as the "Air India furor." I would imagine that the investigators at the time wanted to prevent a repeat performance as well as determine who was behind the bombing.

This last point bears comment. Despite the relative lack of successful attacks anywhere after Air India, Sikh terrorism has not disappeared completely. Sikhs wanting an independent homeland have not achieved their goal after all.

Furthermore, in its 2019 annual report, Public Safety Canada wrote:

> Some individuals in Canada continue to support Sikh (Khalistani) extremist ideologies and movements. This political movement aims to create an independent homeland for Sikhs called Khalistan, in India. Violent activities in

support of an independent Sikh homeland have fallen since their height during the 1982–1993 period when individuals and groups conducted numerous terrorist attacks. The 1985 Air India bombing by Khalistani terrorists, which killed 331 people, remains the deadliest terrorist plot ever launched in Canada. While attacks around the world in support of this movement have declined, support for the extreme ideologies of such groups remains. For example, in Canada, two key Sikh organisations, Babbar Khalsa International and the International Sikh Youth Federation, have been identified as being associated with terrorism and remain listed terrorist entities under the Criminal Code.

In a late August 2020 article in the *National Post* (a right of centre Canadian newspaper) it was claimed that tensions surrounding an independent Khalistan for the Sikhs are still high in Canada. Men in a truck decked out in Indian flags, who were apparently armed, approached an anti-India demonstration in Brampton (just outside of Toronto) seeking to meet the promoter of the event, who earlier claimed to have received death threats.[22]

Former Indian Prime Minister Manmohan Singh, on a visit to Toronto in 2010, told an audience, "there are, however, some elements outside India, including in Canada, who try to keep this issue alive for their own purposes. In many cases, such elements have links to or are themselves wedded to terrorism."[23]

Alleged Canadian Sikh extremists are still on no-fly lists as of 2020. As reported by Canadian reporter Stewart Bell of Global News in 2020, two men were placed on the list at some point around 2017 for "promoting extremism, including the radicalisation of youth, with the aim of achieving Khalistan independence; and attack planning and facilitation, including weapons procurement, to conduct attacks in India."[24]

And it is not just in Canada that pro-Khalistan terrorists are active. In September 2020 Indian police in the state of Punjab announced that it had broken a two-person terrorist cell that was cooperating with known criminals, including one imprisoned in Amritsar.[25] While it is prudent to take what Indian authorities have to say about Sikh extremism with a grain of salt, it is still a fact that the movement for independence in India is not dead and that there are inevitably elements that will seek to establish their goals violently.

As recently as the summer of 2020 the Hindu nationalist government of Indian Prime Minister Narendra Modi was still showing signs of concern over the push for an independent Khalistan. It took steps to delete tweets posted by the Canada-based World Sikh Organisation (WSO) that recalled what the latter terms the 1984 "genocide" of Sikhs and even blocked the hashtag #Sikh on Facebook and Instagram for a period of time.[26]

I learned, however, that the Sikh investigation actually continued until the late 1990s and only ended once the investigation of Islamist extremism began to require more CT resources. There were other events about which CSIS was worried. The reason for this should not be hard to fathom: the Canadian government could not be seen to be lax on the investigation of a terrorist movement behind the single greatest attack in history in terms of loss of life. If CSIS had shunted Sikh terrorism aside and another attack had taken place, one contact told me that would have been the end of the organisation.

The Sikh investigation was truly a national one as the Service uncovered plots in several cities. It should be noted, however, that Sikh extremists physically assaulted former British Columbia Premier Ujjal Dosanjh in 1985—before the Air India bombing—for speaking out against an independent Khalistan.

There was another attack. On May 25, 1986, Malkiat Singh Sidhu, a Minister of State in the Gandhi cabinet, was ambushed on a dirt road—he had come to Canada, unbeknownst to Canadian officials, to attend his nephew's wedding—when four gunmen, members of the ISYF, shot him twice and fled. The gunmen were stopped at a roadblock, arrested, and charged with attempted murder. At the trial, a defence lawyer argued that the CSIS warrant application had not followed procedures and the case was dismissed. A government appeal led to a retrial and the convictions were eventually upheld.

As an interesting side note, one which the current Trudeau government would probably like to forget, one of the four convicted in the terrorist attack, Jaspal Atwal, was later found on an invitation list for a dinner for the prime minister during a state visit to India in 2018. Atwal had also been charged in the aforementioned attack on British Columbia Premier Dosanjh but was acquitted.

I also learned that when Canada hosted a Commonwealth Heads of Government Meeting (CHOGM) in Vancouver in 1987, there were concerns that Indian Prime Minister Rajiv Gandhi would be targeted by Sikh terrorists. Preventing that from happening, from an intelligence collection angle, became the CSIS number one priority. As it turned out, no such attack took place.

Nevertheless, there was a silver lining to the presence of Sikh terrorists in Canada in the 1980s insofar as the development of CSIS as an intelligence service is concerned. As a contact who worked on these investigations during that time told me, following Air India, there was a concerted effort on the part of the Sikh desk (investigative unit) at CSIS HQ to provide direction and tasking to the Service's regional offices to focus on the recruitment of quality human sources inside the Sikh terrorist movement. In many cases, these efforts proved more successful than could ever have been imagined.

CSIS human source recruitment allowed the Service to gain access to individuals at the highest levels within some Sikh terrorist groups, to share vital, real-time intelligence with allied services allowing them to act, and to stop several terrorist attacks that were in their operational phase, originating in Pakistan and aimed at India across the border. All of these planned attacks were the work of Canadian Sikh terrorists.

More importantly, during this period CSIS changed from a predominately CI organization to one that devoted significant resources to CT programs. Sikh terrorism remained the Service's number one priority throughout this time. Between 1985 and 1990, CSIS officers working the Sikh target evolved into internationally recognised experts in the field and constantly liaised with allied services and presented their perspective on this international threat. CSIS received many commendations from allied services for the expert quality of its presentations as well as its contribution to the overall allied understanding of the international threat. Often what CSIS knew was unique and stemmed from the recruitment of high-level sources in Sikh terrorist groups.

At the same time, human source coverage inside Canada allowed the Service to mount operations domestically (often through confrontational interviews) that served to mitigate the Sikh threat in this country. As my contact noted, this is the real story of the investigation of Sikh terrorism in Canada. CSIS transformed itself from a small, underfunded group of former Mounties into an internationally recognised intelligence organisation that punched above its weight and was able to provide real-time intelligence to stop terrorist attacks abroad and mitigate the risk domestically. It was this baseline of expertise that allowed CSIS to quickly react and develop sources and intelligence regarding Islamist terrorism long before it became a global threat (to be discussed in the next chapter).

Nevertheless, all things being considered, I do not believe there was an active Sikh terrorism investigation anywhere in Canada when I retired from CSIS in 2015. That could of course change if events dictate so. After all, we want our security services to be proactive, not reactive.

In closing it bears repeating that we, as a security intelligence community, failed on June 23, 1985. We did not have information that Air India Flight 182 was going to be targeted but we did know that there was a significant Sikh extremist presence in Canada. We should have done better. We did not.

As one highly-placed contact told me: "This should not have happened."

Iranian Terrorism

The year 1979 was a seminal one in the development of modern terrorism. Three events in three different countries unfolded—Afghanistan, Saudi Arabia, and Iran—each of which made a tremendous contribution to terrorism and terrorist movements. One of them is of direct relevance to this section.

On Boxing Day of that year, Soviet forces moved into Afghanistan to support a puppet communist government. Not having learned the lesson from the 19th century that Afghanistan has deservedly been called the "graveyard of empires," the USSR decided to overstay their welcome and, in all senses, occupy the country. After a long, complex set of encounters and battles the Soviets decided to withdraw a decade later, a rag-tag Afghan/Arab bunch with significant US military aid had defeated a much larger army and some of the victors morphed into Al Qaeda.

The second great event of 1979 goes largely unremarked but in hindsight was a very important marker in the development of modern Islamist terrorism In November of that year a group of Saudi Islamist extremists took over the Grand Mosque in Mecca and held out against security forces for two weeks. These terrorists espoused a very intolerant and narrow interpretation of Islam, formed in part by the Wahhabist tradition in Saudi Arabia itself. Following the end of the siege, inexplicably, the Kingdom did not crack down on the fundamentalist views that created the siege: Saudi-influenced Islam has helped feed Islamist terrorism ever since.

But it is the third event that is of direct relevance here. In February of 1979, the rule of the Shah of Iran came to an end and a theocratic government led by Ayatollah Khomeini took its place. Iran has not been the same since.

The Shia clerics who wanted to establish a "government of God" were not the only ones in opposition to the despotic regime of the Shah. Student groups, unions, leftists, and others, all made a contribution to the overthrow of the Pahlavi dynasty and were largely thrown aside once Ayatollah Khomeini made his triumphant return from exile in Paris.

The Mujahideen-e-Khalq (MeK)

One of those groups goes by the name Mujahideen-e-Khalq (MeK), the People's Mujahideen of Iran (sometimes rendered MKO for Mujahideen-e-Khalq Organisation). This is a leftist group that is best seen as a cult, one devoted to its two founders, Massoud and Maryam Rajavi.

The Rajavis have imposed bizarre rituals on members such as gender segregation (even among spouses) and the requirement to engage in public confessions. The membership's allegiance to the couple is legendary and was in part what drove a terrorist attack in Canada.

Once the MeK realised it had no place in the Khomeinist regime it began to target the latter through acts of violence. The best-known attack occurred in 1981 when the group detonated bombs inside the head office of the Islamic Republic Party and the Premier's office, killing some seventy high-ranking Iranian officials, including Chief Justice Ayatollah Mohammad Beheshti, President Mohammad-Ali Rajaei, and Premier Mohammad-Javad Bahonar.

Not surprisingly, Iran sees the MeK as a terrorist organisation, as did Canada for the longest time. The Iranian regime put a lot of pressure on the group, arresting and executing many members, and by the late 1980s the organisation decamped to Iraq, where Iraqi President/dictator Saddam Hussein was only too happy to house an enemy of his enemy. Following the US invasion of Iraq in 2003 the MeK were forced to stay at Camp Ashraf and have since essentially disappeared from most people's radar.

On April 5, 1992, MeK supporters in ten Western countries attacked and pillaged Iranian embassies in the wake of rumours of an Iranian bombing of one of its bases north of Baghdad.[27] News spread that the National Liberation Army (NLA) had been hit, followed by false rumours that the Rajavis had been killed. Enraged at the believed loss of their lead couple, MeK adherents went on a rampage.

On this day, the Iranian embassy in Ottawa was one of the locations targeted. Thirty-five people stormed the embassy and caused a lot of physical damage; the ambassador and an Iranian seeking to have some paperwork completed were injured, but no one was killed. Twenty-eight of the assailants were arrested.

I was at CSE working as a Farsi linguist and Iranian analyst when this attack unfolded. I had been studying the MeK for some time and had even collected literature from one of their sidewalk kiosks in the late 1980s in Toronto (for research purposes of course!). That the group was capable of instigating action on this scale was somewhat surprising.

Other Canadian security agencies had a legitimate interest in the MeK presence in Canada, but after conducting investigations for some time, the effort was proving to deliver little in terms of threat intelligence. Until the attack in 1992. The running joke was that whenever management was considering ending efforts against the MeK, the group would do something rash, forcing us to keep looking at them. I knew one of the security community's lead investigators on the MeK and could sense her frustration at having to keep looking at these actors.

A similar event occurred almost a decade later, forcing us to keep looking at the MeK. In the aftermath of a decision by the French government to arrest Maryam Rajavi, the latter's followers set themselves on fire around the world. A young woman from Ottawa, Neda Hassani, died from her burns after she set herself alight on June 19, 2003.[28] Besides Hassani, seven other people set themselves on fire: those who died were seen as martyrs by the group. In addition, approximately 1,000 people in France (and a dozen or so in Ottawa) went on hunger strikes. France elected to release Rajavi on July 3 of that year.

The MeK was listed as a terrorist entity in the very first such document in Canada after 9/11 (see introduction), due to the terrorist nature of the group. Then, just before Christmas Day in 2012, the Harper government "delisted" them, apparently following the lead of the European Union and the US.

It is hard to imagine why this move was made. It is entirely possible that it was indeed predicated on what our allies had done: Canada is often a follower, and not a leader, in these matters. Yet it smacks of politics as well. No one would say that the current Iranian regime is in any way helpful: they meddle in the affairs of neighbours and are of course the main sponsor of Hizballah, often called the "A-team" of terrorism.

Was this a case of seeing the MeK more as freedom fighters than as terrorists? Was this an example of "the enemy of my enemy is my friend"? The US offered the excuse that they elected to remove the MeK from the list as it had not "not engaged in terrorism for more than a decade." Under that line of reasoning Canada should delist Aum Shinrikyo as well: it has been inactive for twenty-five years! It is of interest that the Conservative government offered no reasons for its decision.[29]

To my mind this seems to be a political decision at heart. And this speaks to what terrorism has become: a political football. The MeK is still a terrorist group in my view, albeit one that is far from the level of groups such as ISIS and AQ, and perhaps not warranting more than a watching brief. But to say it no longer constitutes a violent extremism entity undermines everything that agencies like CSIS stand for. I can assure you that decisions made by politicians and senior mandarins can often rankle those who work in counterterrorism.

Mansour Ahani

But it is not just Iranian oppositionists who have planned terrorist attacks in Canada. The Iranian regime has as well, at least on one occasion. And it was thanks to CSIS that it failed to accomplish its task.

In 1988 the novel *The Satanic Verses* by UK author Salman Rushdie was published. Although not an easy read in my opinion (I tried!), what helped it shoot to fame was the subsequent death threats Rushdie received, many of which originated with the Iranian government. The ayatollahs concluded that parts of the book, especially a dream sequence involving the Prophet Muhammad, were insulting to Muslims. Several fatwas (Islamic religious rulings) were issued calling on true believers to kill the apostate Rushdie: indeed, a Japanese translator of Satanic Verses was killed and an Italian publisher who issued the book was stabbed.

Extremists' obsession with Rushdie has not dissipated. On August 12, 2022 Rushdie was stabbed and seriously injured while giving a talk in Chataqua, New York. His assailant was identified as a 24-year old American of Lebanese origin and police speculated there was a religious motivation to the attack.

Which brings us to the plot in Canada.

In December 1992 Rushdie was scheduled to speak at an event hosted by PEN, a worldwide organisation of writers, in Toronto. Canadian officials were not made aware of Rushdie's travel despite the obvious threat.

Waiting for the writer was Mansour Ahani, an Iranian assassin sent by the Iranian Ministry of Intelligence and Security (MOIS) to kill him. MOIS's fingerprints had also been found on other plots around the world.

Except that Ahani claimed to be a refugee fleeing the Iranian regime. As a consequence, he could receive protection from Canada and not be deported to his native land for fear of mistreatment: torture and death. He travelled from Vancouver, where he made his application for refugee status, to Toronto, where he began working at a Burger King which happened to be near the Winter Garden Theatre where the PEN event was to take place.

What happened next seems to be right out of a spy novel. The account I present here is derived from reporting by Stewart Bell who was with the *National Post* at the time,[30] but it was confirmed by a CSIS contact who worked on the case.

As a side note, I too had a small part to play in the affair. I recall getting a phone call from a CSIS liaison officer at 2 a.m. one day asking me to go to the office at CSE to "have a look at something." Sensitivity precludes me from going into any detail but suffice to say it was tied to the plot to kill Rushdie.

Ahani was being run as an agent by the MOIS. He travelled extensively, was known to have taken part in an attack on Iranian dissidents in Pakistan and went to Switzerland using a false Andorran passport under the name Pablo Gomes, to meet his MOIS handler. It is believed he was there to get instructions on killing other Iranian dissidents in Italy. He was arrested by Italian police but released due to a lack of evidence.

Returning to Canada, this time on a false Greek passport, Ahani was picked up by CSIS and taken to a resort north of Toronto to be interviewed, where he admitted that he was an MOIS assassin. Rushdie was not in danger, although police presence at the PEN affair was high: CSIS had done its job.

Ahani was arrested and charged with terrorism offences in 1993. He tried to use the fear of torture to avoid deportation to Iran, but following several appeals was eventually sent back to Iran in 2002. It is unknown what became of him afterwards.

This case illustrates several aspects of counterterrorism in Canada. Firstly, it was one of the only "state-sponsored" plots aimed at Canada in our history of which I am aware. The investigations I worked on were all planned or executed (or both), by groups or individuals, not states.

Secondly, it showed that CSIS can work with foreign partners to share and receive intelligence related to terrorist threats and act in advance of actual terrorist acts. Thirdly, it pointed to the age-old attempt by terrorists to try to use the "torture clause" to prevent their removal from Canada. This topic will be taken up in much more detail in the penultimate chapter.

All in all, this was a success for the security community and Canada in the prevention of a terrorist attack in Toronto. As we will see in the next chapter, a much bigger attack in that city was also thwarted thanks in part to this same community.

Summary

All the extremist campaigns discussed in this chapter have an underlying commonality: none of the groups and individuals who elected to use violence to achieve a form of national independence or inflict punishment on a government to right historic wrongs have achieved their goals. The Irish terrorists still see Northern Ireland as not part of the Republic of Ireland. French Canadian extremists still see Quebec as not part of Canada. Armenian terrorists have not convinced successive Turkish governments to apologise for the 1915 genocide: the recent victory by Azeri troops in Nagorno-Karabakh over Armenia, facilitated in part with Turkish military assistance, will add to Armenian recriminations against Turkey. Sikh terrorists do not have an independent Khalistan. The MeK still hate to see the Ayatollahs in charge of Iran.

In other words, none of these players can point to their use of violence as having achieved much, if anything at all. This series of failures can lead to two opposing future directions:

a) The realisation that terrorism does not work, in that it does not convince those seen as responsible for obstacles in the path of whatever the terrorist groups are trying to achieve to alter their behaviour. This could push those in these groups, as well as supporters, and the rest who never did sign on, to opt for alternative methods to obtain the same goals—negotiations, conferences, dialogue, etc.

b) a renewed sense of purpose under the delusion that violence will eventually work, if only efforts were redoubled.

In the latter instance it is therefore not impossible that Canada, as a nation which welcomes thousands of individuals from the ethno-nationalist communities discussed in this chapter, may resurrect the kinds of terrorist actions examined here. I am not saying that it is likely, merely that it is possible.

If indeed we were to see fresh campaigns of violence along these lines it would be incumbent upon CSIS and the RCMP to relaunch investigations to follow these actors, recruit and run human sources into their midsts, and carry out surveillance to neutralise any terrorist plans. In light of the time lag in some cases since the last active efforts against these groups, there would be a learning curve of sorts to manage. We should hope that there are individuals within these agencies who remember "the old days" or that veterans could be brought in to advise the new generation as to the nature of these threats. After all, no one wants to see another successful attack on the scale of Air India in 1985.

3

Islamist Terrorism

Canada's officially become one of our enemies by fighting and bombing us and creating a lot of terror in our countries and killing us and killing our innocents."
- Michael Zehaf-Bibeau, Ottawa terrorist, October 22, 2014

This is a message to Canada and all the tawagheet [infidels]: we are coming and we will destroy you.

- Farah Shirdon, ISIS terrorist

IN THIS CHAPTER WE WILL LOOK AT the phenomenon of Islamist extremism from a Canadian perspective, that is, terrorist acts in which Canadians played a part, both in Canada and abroad.

This chapter is by far the longest in this book on terrorism in Canada over the past century and a half. This is so for three primary reasons: Islamist terrorism is the subject with which I am most familiar, having focused on the issue while working at CSIS for thirteen years, and written five books on the topic to date; this form of violent extremism, as of today, represents the single greatest terrorist threat to this country and to the world; and the sheer number of terrorist plots in which Canadians played a role—both in Canada and abroad—warrant attention.

Two other aspects of how this chapter is organised bear mentioning. First, I have elected to divide the history of Islamist terrorism into three distinct periods, as outlined below.

- Pre-9/11. Even if the phrase "the post-9/11 period" is a bit hackneyed it does serve to illustrate how terrorism attracted greater resources in Canada and led to the creation of whole new bodies to deal with it, when compared to the "pre-9/11 period."
- Post-9/11 to 2013. This time frame coincides with my years at CSIS and is thus a period in which I had full and unfettered access to all intelligence gathered in the course of counterterrorism investigations.
- Post-2013. During this time, I was no longer part of the investigative world (initially due to a secondment to the

National Security Directorate at Public Safety Canada and then to retirement from the public service). As a result, all the information to be discussed is derived from open sources.

Finally, while the (planned) attacks, similarly to those in the last chapter, will be discussed as close to chronologically as possible, I have decided to organise them into three categories:

a) Attacks planned or carried out by Canadians in Canada.
b) Attacks planned or carried out by Canadians outside of Canada.
c) Canadian foreign fighters, i.e., those who joined terrorist groups abroad but who were not linked to explicit attack planning (there are a few cases, such as that of Salman Ashrafi of Calgary, Alberta, which constitute both b) and c)).

I have endeavoured to include major characters or plots in this chapter. From 2001 to 2013, I worked on somewhere between 300 and 400 investigations carried out by Canadian security agencies on Islamist extremism in Canada. This constitutes a lot of data! That not all led to plots or arrests is not relevant. The whole purpose of an investigation is to determine if there is any real threat which would warrant more in-depth inquiries should matters take a more worrisome turn.

The significance of this number should not go unnoticed. Simply stated, the examination of individuals and groups in Canada who espouse a hateful and intolerant (as well as non-normative) interpretation of Islam which calls for the use of violence has been by far the number one priority for the Canadian security intelligence and law enforcement community when it comes to terrorism for the past two decades. It is not possible to argue otherwise or to maintain that resources should have been redeployed elsewhere, a point I will return to in the next chapter.

Many of these cases were discussed in my book *The Threat From Within*. In this volume I have elected to summarise the cases presented there, updated with new information, commentary and reflections. I hope that the added context provides interesting and valuable insight into Islamist terrorism in Canada.

With these explanatory remarks out of the way, let us turn our attention to what some call "jihadi terrorism" in Canada.

The Pre-9/11 Period

In conversations with several former CSIS counterterrorism agents and source handlers I learned that while Islamist extremism was not a priority in the mid to late 1980s—that was reserved for Sikh terrorism in the wake of Air India as previously discussed, and, to a lesser extent, Armenian extremism—this form of terrorism was not ignored completely. The security intelligence community was looking at several terrorist groups that functioned primarily abroad: Palestinian groups were of particular interest.

Furthermore, the development of AQ in Afghanistan after the Soviet invasion of that nation in 1979 was being monitored. The security intelligence community also kept an eye on what was happening in North Africa, especially after the decision by the Algerian military annulled an election in 1992 when it was clear that an Islamist party was going to win. Canada has a large Maghrebi population and, as we will see, Canadians originally from that part of the world have taken part in terrorist acts both here and abroad.

Over the years, the ways in which CSIS chose to divide its counterterrorism coverage changed frequently. At the headquarters level there were once "South Asian" and "North African" sections, each responsible for that part of the globe. At the regional level, this split would be managed differently, depending on the size of that office. For instance, the Toronto and Montreal offices are significantly larger than the Winnipeg and Fredericton ones, necessitating a different approach.

Once 9/11 happened much was altered yet again. The need to divide terrorism into geographic swathes no longer seemed as important. And, as we will see, there were dozens of plots and hundreds of investigations that unfolded, all of which were complicated in their own right. Earlier ways of carving up the terrorism pie were not feasible.

We will now continue to look at specific terrorism cases that arose in the pre-9/11 period.

The Curious Case of Hassan Diab

On October 3, 1980, a motorcycle bomb believed to have been left by members of the Popular Front for the Liberation of Palestine (PLFP), a secular (not jihadi) Marxist group founded in 1967, killed four people and wounded more than forty outside a synagogue on rue Copernic in Paris.

There was no sound of an explosion, just the clattering of glass, the screaming of children and the groaning of bloodied adults in states of semi-consciousness. "The glass came down on our heads. The door flew off its hinges. Then a ball of flame lit the synagogue. That was the petrol tanks of the cars exploding."[31]

There is a fascinating sideline to this attack involving a man, Hassan Diab, who teaches at the University of Ottawa, where I am currently a Distinguished Fellow in National Security within the Professional Development Institute. Diab has fought a decades-long battle to clear his name with French judicial authorities who say he is the prime suspect in this attack. However, he says he was not in Paris at the time and that the French case against him is based on shoddy police work and bad intelligence. Not surprisingly, the French think differently.[32]

As of the time of writing, Diab is suing the Canadian government for $90 million in damages for its role in aiding the French government in its investigation of him as well as for his extradition to France where he spent three years in solitary confinement pending their continued efforts to find how he was linked to the attack. A judge concluded in 2018 that the case had no merit and returned Diab to Canada. The French government is appealing that decision. In light of the status of this case—it is before the courts—I will refrain from further comment. Stay tuned.

The Jamaat ul-Fuqra Plot

One of the more bizarre terrorist plots unfolded in Toronto in 1991 when a cell of individuals belonging to the Pakistani group Jamaat ul-Fuqra (JuF, also known in North America as Muslims of America) planned to bomb a Hindu temple and theatre. The act was interdicted when several of the cell members were arrested at the Rainbow Bridge crossing between Canada and the US in the Niagara Peninsula and detailed plans were discovered to target the India Centre cinema in Toronto (capacity 500) and the Vishnu Hindu temple in Richmond Hill (capacity 4,000) during the Hindu Festival of Lights, a time when many Canadian Hindus would be present.[33]

I will admit that sometimes luck plays a role in good intelligence and in helping to stop bad things from happening. The aforementioned stop on the Rainbow Bridge was the first indication that something was afoot. In other words, the plot had not been detected by the security intelligence community, at least according to a contact who was working in Toronto at the time. Nevertheless, the information seized was acted upon and no attack took place. This incident is an excellent real-life example of the IRA's taunting of the UK years ago: "You have to get lucky 100 percent of the time; we have to get lucky once." Indeed, we got lucky this time.

There are several aspects of this early plot that bear commentary and I have some interesting personal experiences to share as well. Most of the terrorists involved were converts to Islam, some Trinidadians and some Dominicans (from the Caribbean island of Dominica, not Dominican priests!). One of the leaders, a Trinidadian by the name of Glenn Neville Ford, had come to Canada in the 1970s and founded a JuF branch here in the 1980s. He also travelled to Pakistan to meet JuF leader Shaikh Gilani, who was later tied to the killing of Wall Street Journal reporter Daniel Pearl in 2002.

In the end, eight terrorists were arrested and five went to trial in St. Catharines, Ontario. They were acquitted of terrorism but three, including Tyrone Cole (more on him in a bit) were convicted of "conspiring to commit mischief endangering life." They were jailed and upon completion of their sentence all deported (none were Canadian citizens).

Here is where my personal anecdote comes in. I spend vacations at a cottage on a small lake in the Madawaska Highlands of Ontario, an hour or so east of the internationally renowned Algonquin Park. Less than half an hour's drive from this place is the small town of Combermere, on the shores of Lake Kamineskeg. Just outside Combermere is a hamlet called Hasanville—it does not usually show up on maps—which was set up by Ford and others as a compound.

Despite its origins, Hasanville has not made the news for any extremist activity and this case has become largely forgotten in Canada.

In the mid-2000s, just after Tyrone Cole and two others were deported from Canada, I travelled to Kingston, Ontario, sometimes called "prison town" because of the concentration of penitentiaries located there, to meet with officials to talk about radicalisation to violence. A security intelligence officer confided to me that under Cole's direction some fifty inmates had converted to Islam. I am not saying that this is the same as fifty inmates adopting Islamist extremist ideology, but it cannot help when the person's gateway to the faith is himself an Islamist terrorist.

The issue of radicalisation in prison is one that preoccupies many security services around the world. In my time at CSIS I met with officials across Canada as well as in many other nations. The UK and France in particular have a huge problem in this regard. Authorities struggle with how to house terrorist inmates: do they keep them all together so they can reinforce each other or spread them out to avoid this but risk the "contamination" of other prisoners. A hard problem to be sure.

The last part of this story is what happened after Cole was deported. He was returned to his native Trinidad and Tobago where he established a fortified JuF compound in Port of Spain. I met with the Trinidadian Security Service in the early 2010s and was apprised that Cole and his cohort were a real headache for them. Suffice to say that twenty years in a Canadian jail did not seem to douse the flames of jihad for this terrorist.

In the end, it was instructive that terrorism charges were not upheld. In the early 1990s we in Canada were simply not that good at gaining convictions in terrorism cases and, in all honesty, have had a mixed record since then. I will return to this point in the penultimate chapter.

(As an aside, I discuss this plot in a blog on my website's "Today in Terrorism" series.[34])

Kassem Daher

In his 2004 book *Cold Terror*, Canadian journalist Stewart Bell provided insight into Kassem Daher, an Alberta resident who ended up arrested in his native Lebanon in 2002. Bell even interviewed Daher in Beirut where the latter denied ever being involved in "extremism," for which Lebanese authorities picked him up. Utter hogwash.

As Bell suggests in his book, Kassem Daher was a major Islamist extremist figure in Western Canada in the 1990s. It is not an exaggeration to state that he was the prominent radicaliser for many across Canada for the better part of a decade. It would not be surprising if most cases of Islamist extremism investigated by Canadian security agencies in the 1990s were determined to have had some link to Daher. Some of the connections might be significant, some less so. Still, Daher posed a threat to Canadian public safety in his role as a type of éminence grise, a man lurking in the shadows doling out inspiration and religious guidance to others. While it is difficult to determine how many went on to actually do anything violent, either here or abroad, the scale of Daher's influence cannot be underestimated. He was a linchpin, and not just in Canada according to one of my contacts. That he lived in the small city of Leduc, Alberta, merely underscores that extremism can happen anywhere.

What Daher represented is something that tends to be dismissed in the conversation about Islamist extremism. We usually focus our attention and energy on those who plan or commit acts of terrorism, and rightly so as security intelligence and law enforcement agencies are tasked with identifying and preventing things from going boom in the night. But it is also vital to consider those who sit back and plant the seed. Called "radicalisers" or "influencers," these individuals play a vital role in providing religious justification and moral support or encouragement to the bomb chuckers. The role that the bedrock of faith plays—as evidenced in almost every single piece of propaganda issued by terrorist groups such as AQ and ISIS—explains in large part why clerics are often found playing these roles. While not technically an Islamic preacher, Daher filled that position for years.

To quote a CSIS agent who testified at a security certificate hearing in the early 2000s, "It is our (CSIS) assessment . . . that anybody who had significant contact with Mr. Kassem Daher would likely be part of that particular Islamic extremist organisation."[35]

Here's hoping Daher is not allowed back to Canada any time soon.

The Khadr Family

The year was 1996. Then Canadian Prime Minister Jean Chretien was on a trade mission to Pakistan when he met Canadian citizen Maha Al Samnah whose husband, Ahmed Said Khadr, was being held by the government of Benazir Bhutto on suspicion of involvement in the November 1995 terrorist attack on the Egyptian Embassy in Islamabad in which seventeen people, including an Egyptian diplomat, were killed and another sixty injured. Prime Minister Chretien asked his Pakistani counterpart to ensure that Khadr receive fair treatment, even posing for a picture with him in a hospital. Khadr was soon released.

On the surface, this was a run-of-the-mill act by a Canadian official (albeit the prime minister!) in aid of a fellow citizen. In this case, however, Khadr was a known associate of AQ leader Usama bin Laden—a "most wanted" terrorist in a list drawn up by the US after 9/11—and the head of a Canada-based charity in Pakistan and Afghanistan known as Human Concern International (HCI). That an extremist would use a humanitarian organisation as a cover for his real activities and travel to global hotspots was an important finding for the security services.

My own connection to HCI is minor but of potential interest. I lived a kilometre away from their headquarters in a non-descript building near an industrial park in the eastern part of Ottawa. That area is also just down the street from where I played hockey for three decades. I therefore drove by HCI three or four times a week on my way to the arena. I always found it fascinating that an organisation used by a Canadian jihadi to hide his real activities was part of my very Canadian neighbourhood and along my commute to engage in a very Canadian activity. How more Canadian can you get?

The bottom line is that it would be reasonable to assume that Khadr was using a Canadian-registered charity to fund a terrorist group. And our government, in the form of the prime minister, went to bat for him. Oh my.

If you want to start an argument in Canada over those who think we are not tough enough on terrorism and those who are convinced our security services run roughshod on human rights, just raise the case of Omar Khadr, son of Ahmed Said Khadr. The former was seized by American forces in Afghanistan in 2002 after he killed a US medic. He was fifteen years old at the time.

Khadr junior was taken to Guantanamo Bay and held there for a decade. While in custody he was questioned not just by the Americans but also by CSIS officials on what he knew about Canadian Islamist extremists in Afghanistan and Pakistan. Then the proverbial shit hit the fan.

Those who support Omar Khadr demanded his immediate release from Gitmo. They called him a child soldier and said that Canada was remiss in not repatriating him to our country. Omar Khadr sued his own government and in 2010 the Supreme Court ruled that Canada had "offend[ed] the most basic Canadian standards [of] the treatment of detained youth suspects." He returned to Canada in 2012 after pleading guilty to "murder in the violation of the law of war" in a US hearing to finish his sentence in a Canadian prison. In 2017 the government awarded him $10.5 million in damages for the violation of his rights under the Canadian Charter of Rights and Freedoms. He is now a free man.

Canadians were divided on this issue. A 2017 poll by the Canadian Broadcasting Corporation demonstrated that 71 percent of those asked opposed the settlement.[36] Still, Omar Khadr has become a hero to some here in Canada. As in most things in life, the reality is a little more complicated.

At its most fundamental point, CSIS was absolutely authorised and mandated to question Omar Khadr in Guantanamo. The legality (and image) of that facility notwithstanding, CSIS had to interrogate Omar Khadr to see what he knew about threats to Canada's national security as well as that of its allies. As the son of an AQ leader he could have been privy to information related to attack planning here or abroad. It is not unreasonable to assume that the Khadr family head could have shared details with his progeny around the dinner table. Furthermore, Omar and his siblings were raised in part in AQ training camps and would most likely have come to know other terrorists, possibly other Canadian terrorists.

Omar Khadr and the rest of his family were supporters of former AQ leader Usama bin Laden. As a consequence, CSIS and other security agencies had a duty to collect intelligence on the family in any way possible to be in a position to inform the Canadian government on threats to national security and public safety. Omar Khadr's case may be a special one in light of his stay at the controversial prison at Camp X-Ray, but there can be no doubt that his family posed a threat to us and others.

We will see other cases of family members who opted to become terrorists together but nothing on the scale of the Khadrs (even daughter Zaynab showed her true colours to Canadians in a televised interview in 2004 ....[37]). Let's hope we never see another such group of Canadian extremists.

Here is another Khadr story. In 2003, Toronto lawyer Rocco Galati elected to represent one member of the Khadr clan, Abdurahman, who had been released from Guantanamo Bay. At a press conference upon his return to Canada, Galati smugly sat in the background as reporters peppered the Khadr offspring with questions. Galati and others undoubtedly thought that the terrorism allegations against the Khadrs were false and were using the questionable decision to incarcerate alleged terrorists in Guantanamo as fodder.

In response to a question, Khadr stated that he had spent some time at a place called "Khalden." Galati's face visibly dropped. He seemed to realise what his client had said. Khalden was a known AQ training camp, and anyone there would have been part of a terrorist group. Oops.

Galati later dropped Khadr as a client when—or at least according to him—he received a death threat for daring to represent a terrorist ("Well, Mr. Galati. What's this I hear about you working with the terrorist now, helping to get that punk terrorist Khadr off. Now you a dead wop."[38]). All

I know is that those of us who were working counterterrorism at the time and watched the press conference had to smile at this interesting turn in events.

OK, one more Khadr story. Last one, I promise. Jean Chretien was not the only prime minister to get caught up with the family. In 2019, Zainab Khadr's ex-husband, Joshua Boyle, returned to Canada after having been held by the Taliban in Afghanistan for five years. He and his new wife, Caitlin Coleman, were supposedly hiking in that country when they were seized. They returned to Canada in 2017 and Boyle had an (in)famous meeting with Justin Trudeau in the prime minister's office. A few days later, Coleman alleged that her husband had sexually assaulted her, though the charges were dismissed in 2019.[39]

I am not sure what the Trudeau government was thinking at the time. Why on earth would any government choose a photo-op with anyone linked to the Khadrs? There may also be more to the "backpacking" story in Afghanistan. Some free advice to future Canadian PMs: if the Khadrs come calling, don't answer the door!

Ahmed Ressam

In the immediate aftermath of 9/11 the top priority for CSIS and its partners in Canada, in addition to helping our US allies in their investigations on what had happened and who was behind it, was to turn over every rock to determine, and hopefully ensure, that none of the nineteen hijackers had come through Canada.

If it turned out that the hijackers had come through Canada, this would point to problems with our border and immigration systems and indicate that a catastrophic attack on our number one ally had been facilitated, at least in part, by terrorists in Canada. If credible, it would not have been a good day for bilateral relations.

As it turns out, there was another incident in December 1999 that would have been a disaster for Canada and our ties to the US. That was when Ahmed Ressam, a Montreal-based extremist, made it as far as a ferry terminal in Washington state with a car full of explosives heading for Los Angeles International Airport, planning what would be known as the "Millennium attack."

Much is already in the public record about Ressam and does not need to be repeated here. I will focus on two aspects: what CSIS would have known about him and why it failed to stop him, and how a US border agent became a hero that day.

In my interviews with former CSIS agents it was made clear that they were well aware of Ahmed Ressam and his pedigree. They knew he was part of the Algerian terrorist group, the Groupe Islamique Armé (Armed Islamic Group or GIA). He was also known to be part of a criminal gang in Quebec. They knew he had entered Canada on a fake passport, though other officials dismissed the importance of this by maintaining that lots of legitimate refugee claimants did the same. Ressam claimed refugee status and said he would be tortured if sent back to Algeria. They also knew he was an associate of other Islamist terrorists in Canada.

It was also at this time that the phrase "bunch of guys" came to the fore. Canadian security officials saw that the groups of individuals popping up in terrorist investigations were not necessarily tied to specific terrorist organisations abroad or even well-organised in Canada. But, they all sang from the same songsheet—that is, they all professed the same ideology and read the same sources—but they were not a movement with an organisational chart. On the contrary, they were loosely associated cells. In other words, "bunches of guys" or BOGs. For the record, the aforementioned Marc Sageman popularised the term in his 2008 book Leaderless Jihad, although he admitted that he had gotten the phrase from the Canadians.

What is less clear is whether officials knew that Ressam had obtained a Canadian passport using a forged baptismal certificate under the name Benni Noris. He used this false documentation to go to Afghanistan and back, having received training in a camp funded by AQ. It is not certain that officials knew that he had returned in February 1999 as Benni Noris. By the time he went to the West Coast of Canada in November 1999 it seemed the trail had gone cold.

In all honesty it proved difficult to get much detail from my CSIS contacts, and I was not at CSIS at the time of the Ressam affair. Whether this was out of embarrassment that the agency had missed him or that I simply did not talk to the right people is hard for me to ascertain. In any event, the failure to keep tabs on Ressam, despite an investigation over years, and internal warnings that some extremists were taking advantage of Canada's refugee system, was exactly that, a failure. I did learn, however, that there was also some inconsistency within the intelligence community on how to proceed with investigations. This has implications for the tools deployed: surveillance, human source recruitment, warrant applications, etc.

Luckily, we in Canada (and the US) were saved by a very capable US border official. He was questioned by US officials in a pre-clearance facility before boarding a ferry as they were suspicious of him, but they found no grounds to deny him entry. On the ferry, he was again stopped by a US Customs agent who became suspicious of his hesitant answers to her questions. A subsequent search of his car turned up explosives. In response, Ressam made a run for it but was caught and arrested. A year and a bit later he was convicted on nine counts of conspiring to commit a terrorist act.

I would like to think that the US official had intelligence that directed her to focus on Ressam and that some of that intelligence had come originally from Canada, but I cannot state that with any certainty. Maybe there were elements in Ressam's behaviour that raised her suspicion. Maybe she was very well trained on what to pay attention to. In any case, I would assume that seeing an individual bolt from a car once the trunk is open is listed somewhere as a "bad sign." A competent agent saved the day: if Ressam had made it through US Customs there is little chance he would have been stopped before arriving at Los Angeles Airport.

From a Canadian perspective this would have been a disaster. One of my contacts said that the Chretien government was told in blatant terms that the border would be "shut down" if something like this happened again. Given the critical economic relationship Canada enjoys with the US the consequences would have been indescribable.

My contacts also told me that this was CSIS's "9/11 moment." No, the attack did not succeed, but it almost did. CSIS realised it had screwed up and management made it clear that this would not happen again. CT resources were bolstered, and heightened importance was given to counterterrorism. This added attention resulted in a better security service, one that did not have to ramp up completely when 9/11 took place.

One last point, Ressam was linked to an Algerian Canadian named Fateh Kamel who was a lynchpin in recruiting jihadis for the war in Bosnia. I would direct the reader to Stewart Bell's book, *Cold Terror*, which does an excellent job of unraveling the Kamel case.

Post-9/11 to 2013

My memories of 9/11 are crystal clear. As I wrote in my book *An End to the War on Terrorism*, September 11, 2001, was a Tuesday. I had walked to my job at CSIS as was my usual practice. I lived 3.5 km from the office and enjoyed the time there and back in the afternoon/evening to both prepare for the day ahead and process the day's events/get ready for parenting duties awaiting me at home.

The day began as most did: a workout in the CSIS gym followed by my initial daily tasks: checking emails and looking in on what had happened in Canada and internationally overnight, both through the classified intelligence databases as well as open source ones. While engaged in this someone popped their head into my office—yes, I had my own office with a door!—to say that I should come to a common room and look what was on TV. Apparently a plane had just flown into one of the World Trade Center towers in New York.

As I walked to the room it would be disingenuous to try to boast that I had an inkling that this was an act of terrorism. Although I was vaguely aware of AQ—I had written a paper regarding the links between them and the USS Cole bombing in late 2000—I was most definitely NOT a "terrorism expert", a term that is sorely overclaimed and overused. Quite the contrary: my initial thoughts were that this was sadly another case of "pilot error" where a plane tragically flies into a building. These had nothing to do with terrorism, let alone AQ and as a consequence I did not have an 'aha' moment where I knew this was an AQ terrorist attack akin to the 1992 World Trade Center bombing, which was attributable to them.

As I and others were looking up at the screen, a second plane came in from the margins and hit the other tower. Wow! TWO planes that happen to hit the two towers within minutes of each other? And not a single seater Cessna: these were full-bodied airliners. This was no accident: it was deliberate. These had to be acts of terrorism.

After that things go blurry. I was immediately called back to CSE to take my shifts poring through SIGINT intercept to try to figure out what had just happened. More importantly, as the previous look at the Ressam case made clear, we—and here I include my colleagues at CSIS—had to determine whether there was any link to Canada, however tenuous. If there had been (and it soon turned out there were not — phew!) it would have raised uncomfortable questions regarding what our security services were doing (or better yet not doing) and had a significant impact on our relations with the US. The absence of any link did not, however, prevent some, including former Secretary of State and Democratic presidential candidate Hillary Rodham Clinton, from erroneously stating publicly that some of the hijackers came from my country.

To say that everything changed that day is a common, albeit overused, phrase. And yet, that terrorist act did change my career as an intelligence analyst in a big way. After my shifts at CSE ended I convinced my boss to let me go back to CSIS where I increasingly looked at domestic Islamist terrorism. In a sense, then, 9/11 opened the door to a different focus for me, one that has fascinated and challenged me both professionally and even in my 'retirement' years (including this and my other five books on the topic).

As a contact told me, the effect of 9/11 on security intelligence and law enforcement in Canada was the need to shift gears when it came to counterterrorism. Investigations that had been largely focused on Sikhs and Armenians, later Maghrebis and the odd Afghan-linked individuals, now needed to turn to the reality of homegrown terrorism. This was not necessarily an easy thing to do. There was a learning curve.

At the same time, CSIS had been warning the Canadian government that it had been seeing a worrying rise in domestic Islamist extremism over a number of years. In a presentation to the Special Committee of the Senate on Security and Intelligence in 1998, then CSIS Director Ward Elcock stated that CSIS was investigating some 50 organisational targets and 350 individual terrorist targets, and that "Canada's intelligence, police and immigration departments have been warning the Government for years that the world's major terrorist groups had established offshore bases in Canadian cities, and that they were using Canada as a staging ground for political and religious violence around the world."[40] Statements of this type were generally dismissed within other parts of the Canadian government. Many were of the opinion that terrorism of this nature happened "abroad" and was not a major concern for Canada.

As late as 2000, however, the CSIS annual report contained this passage: "The threat from international terrorism will continue to be associated with homeland conflicts. Most terrorist groups have a presence in Canada, and they promote their causes by providing logistical support and safe havens, raising and exporting funds openly or covertly in support of terrorist activities and intimidating immigrant communities into supporting them." Note that this implied that Canadian terrorists would focus their intent outside the country, not inwardly.

In the wake of 9/11, the RCMP and CSIS had to deal with this threat in different ways. As Canada's national police force, the Mounties had to decide whether to shift resources from organised crime and other purely criminal issues to terrorism investigations. An RCMP contact told me that there were constant checks to see that these decisions were the right ones. That organisation also had the option of downloading some tasks to the provinces. For its part, CSIS had to reallocate resources from CI to CT, and more narrowly, homegrown CT (not that CI was dropped: several contacts told me that CSIS retained a robust counter-intelligence effort in the immediate post 9/11 period, one that continues to this day to the best of my knowledge).

When you pivot operations, you run the risk of missing things. There are never enough men and women to do it all. Investigations are never as easy as they look in Hollywood.

This challenge was complicated by a sentiment at higher levels of government within Canada, as noted above, that terrorism really did not matter. One contact told me that senior officials dismissed terrorism as something that happened "over there." If Canadians were leaving to join AQ or raising funds in Canada for Hizballah or the LTTE, those were seen as "not our problem." To say that this is shortsighted and unacceptable is understating the issue. This was despite messaging and briefings by security intelligence and law enforcement agencies that underscored what was being seen through their investigations. To my mind this attitude is tied to a poor intelligence culture in Canada, a point I will return to in the penultimate chapter.

One thing is certain. Resources are always easy to argue for after an incident than before. Once something has gone "boom" everyone wants to throw people and money at a problem. Agencies that are on the receiving end must then decide where to allocate them.

Planned or Successful Acts in Canada

There were four major foiled attacks in Canada in the 9/11 to 2013 period: the Toronto 18 in 2006; Project Samossa [sic] in 2010; and two plots in 2013, the Via Rail plot and the plan to bomb the British Columbia Legislature on Canada Day. We will look at each one separately. Interestingly, there were no successful Islamist terrorist attacks in Canada during this interval (i.e., all were prevented by the efforts of CSIS and the RCMP, and their partners): there were no successful attacks of any ideological stripe as a matter of fact.

The Toronto 18

Sometimes in life we have what is truly a career-changing moment. That instance for me began in the late summer of 2005 when we in the Canadian security intelligence community began to investigate what became by far the largest counterterrorism investigation in our history in the post 9/11 world: what has been called the "Toronto 18." This was a completely homegrown plot to detonate fertiliser bombs at three locations in the Greater Toronto Area. And it turned my job at CSIS around.

In late 2005 intelligence began to trickle in on an individual who stupidly used the online name "C4explosive" and who seemed intent on recruiting like-minded people to engage in terrorist activity. Whether the intent was to attack Canada or to go abroad was not initially clear. Fast forward to June 2, 2006.

The nation's newspapers and websites announced that seventeen men (later eighteen) had been picked up and charged with terrorism. These were not foreigners—they were all Canadian residents. This may have come as a shock to those who were convinced that terrorists were a 'foreign' problem. As more and more information came out Canadians were presented with a set of plots and intrigues, everything from truck bombs to a desire to behead the prime minister. This was without doubt the single biggest terrorism plot on Canadian soil, ever.

At the time of arrest two of the cell members, Saad Gaya and Saad Khalid, were transferring three tonnes of ammonium nitrate from a truck to a storage facility in Toronto. The group also had a working detonator and had likely chosen three targets: near the CSIS office in downtown Toronto, outside the Toronto Stock Exchange, and at an undisclosed Canadian military base (possibly the Trenton Air Force Base, an hour and half east of Toronto). I recall seeing a video illustrating what one tonne of an ammonium nitrate bomb would do: it was not good.

In the end, eleven of the eighteen were either convicted or pleaded guilty to terrorism charges. the other seven were released when the prosecution elected not to pursue their cases. Most of those convicted are now free. One, Alie Dirie, whose story is told in greater detail below, served his sentence and was released, but was not "rehabilitated" and went on to join a terrorist group in Syria, where he died in 2013. That most are free speaks, in my opinion to how serious Canadian courts really see terrorism, and this will be revisited in the penultimate chapter.

Much of the story of the Toronto 18 is known in light of media accounts and court records. In short, the original leader of the group was an Afghan immigrant to Canada named Fahim Ahmad who first came to our attention in the intelligence community because of some of his postings online and the, shall we say 'interesting', usernames ("Soldier of Allah," and "C4explosive"). When confronted by CSIS agents he admitted that the posts were his but that he did not feel it was the "right time" for him to do jihad as he and his wife had a baby girl.

The second major character was Ahmad's bosom buddy, Zakarias Amara, the son of a Christian mother and a Jordanian father who converted to Islam and arrived in Canada with his family at the age of ten. Amara and Ahmad were schoolmates and they also belonged to the Muslim Students Association where they, as well as another member, Saad Khalid, would talk at school of jihad and martyrdom.

Fast forward to December of that year when Ahmad planned an outing in a forest a few hours north of Toronto, where they marched around and fired off a few rounds, pretending to be Chechen mujahideen killing kuffar ("unbelievers"). Thankfully, they were unaware that one of the group was actually a CSIS source, Mubin Shaikh.

By the early 2006, Ahmad and Amara had a falling out as the latter did not think the former was really going to do anything. The group subsequently split. Amara later hooked up with Shareef Abdelhaleem, a successful software engineer but also a radical Islamist.

Abedlhaleem's story is an interesting one as it puts paid to the notion that terrorists are all economic underachievers. According to The Canadian Encyclopedia:

> Before he was an accused terrorist, Shareef Abdelhaleem designed computer databases for drug companies. His salary was six figures, his car was a convertible BMW (metallic blue, with black leather seats), and his boss was everyone's dream boss: himself. "I had a successful career," says Abdelhaleem . . . "God blessed me with a little bit of talent."
>
> God had also blessed him with a big heart, and not only because he shared his Mississauga home with seven stray cats rescued from animal

shelters. Abdelhaleem was literally diagnosed with a growth on his heart, an unusual condition that required major surgery in the spring of 2006. He was still recovering a few weeks later when heavily armed officers stormed through his front door and pinned him to the floor. "To tell you the truth, I wasn't concentrating," he says now, recalling the raid. "I was looking to see if the cats were running out." Days after the bust—days after his name was forever linked to the "Toronto 18"—Abdelhaleem was still fretting about his felines. "Who knows where some of them are now," he says, shaking his head.

Amara used the money from his part-time job at a Canadian Tire gas bar to work on his "project"—a remote-controlled detonator. He later ordered three tons of ammonium nitrate to be used in a truck bomb. Indications are that Amara's wife appeared to have been as extreme as her husband.

Luckily, unbeknownst to Amara and Abdelhaleem, who would chat in the kiosk at the Canadian Tire, the locale was "wired up" to monitor their communications.

As for the other members of the group, they too had their jobs. Stephen Chand, a Hindu convert to Islam born in Fiji, helped with the training at the December camp. Ali Dirie and Yasin Abdi Mohamed went to the US to get guns, but thanks to good intelligence were arrested on their way back to Canada in August 2005. They were both charged and convicted on weapons charges and later charged with terrorism when the cell was rolled up less than a year later. In all, four young offenders were detained and one, Nishanthan Yogakrishnan, was tried as an adult and sentenced to time served.

At the end of it all, here are the sentences which were handed down:

- Fahim Ahmad, 16 years
- Zakarias Amara, life
- Shareef Abdelhaleem, life
- Saad Gaya, 12 years
- Saad Khalid, 20 years
- Ali Dirie, 7 years
- Jahmal James, 7 years (equivalent to time served)
- Steven Chand, 10 years (given credit for 9 years, 4 months)
- Yasin Mohamed, 2 years
- Nishanthan Yogakrishnan, 30 months (equivalent to time served)
- Amin Durrani, 7 1/2 years (equivalent to time served)
- Asad Ansari, 6 years, 5 months (equivalent to time served)

Some of the members of this terrorist cell appear to be trying to reconstruct their lives, which is commendable, but does not negate what they have done. Among these are Saad Gaya, who I understand has graduated from college, and Saad Khalid. I met with both while they were in prison, though secrecy precludes me from conveying what I learned during those meetings.

Suffice to say that releasing convicted terrorists is an important issue that bears on the whole question of radicalisation and de-radicalisation. Many extremists claim that after reconsideration they have dropped their Islamist extremist beliefs and want to rejoin society. Some people buy their stories hook, line, and sinker, and seek to help them regain a sense of a normal life.

I am not of that belief. Maybe this is due to my decades in security intelligence and my exposure to information which clearly indicated that what people said to the outside world and what they said to their like-minded friends was often contradictory. Having access to intelligence provides us with that crucial other side of the story.

If you ask the inmates themselves, no one is actually guilty in prison—they were framed or duped or subject to biased judicial proceedings. What to make of all of this is devilishly hard to know. Attacks in Austria and the UK carried out in 2020 by released jihadi prisoners, some of whom graduated from de-radicalisation programs, are leading many to look at such rehabilitative efforts with a jaundiced eye.

Then there is one member I had occasion to meet after his exit from prison: I have elected to keep his identity secret. He confided that he knew what he had become involved with and believed he had "paid his dues." I got the sense he was being honest with me. He was in effect trying to return to a normal life but this was not easy, as some people still avoided him and securing employment was a challenge. In the end we ceased communicating and I often wondered what became of him.

In essence, the Toronto 18 was keen to punish Canada for its role in sending troops to Afghanistan in the wake of 9/11. They sought to cripple the economy, in part through a massive attack. As the trials took years to make it through the courts a degree of skepticism about how serious the threat was began to surface, especially amongst some in the Muslim communities. Some today still describe the cell as "amateurish", led to act by a CSIS source who later became an RCMP agent. To this way of thinking, they were "the gang that couldn't shoot straight," victims of a sting operation.

There is so much that can be said about this case, enough to constitute a book on its own. However, I will focus on a few items here. With respect to the Muslim communities' skepticism, there is an aspect that has to be mentioned. In a conversation with a CSIS officer who was in Toronto Region at the time of this massive investigation, I learned that he met often with leading community personalities and was accused of an unfair focus on Muslims. "Why didn't you come to us first with your concerns rather than investigate these young men? Now their lives are ruined, and the Muslim community is looked at suspiciously." I have heard this same complaint often in my time at CSIS and as an outreach specialist at Public Safety Canada.

My colleague's response was to ask, "Fair enough, but where were you when these young men talked openly about jihad and their hatred for Canada in your mosques and community centres? How many of you came to us or to the RCMP or to local police with your concerns?" In response he heard "crickets" (i.e., nothing).

While counterterrorism is the purview of CSIS and the RCMP, public safety is the responsibility of all Canadians. I can appreciate hesitation from certain quarters, especially in the cases of new Canadians who come here from countries where security services and law enforcement agencies are not as "friendly" as CSIS and the RCMP. Their objections strike me as shallow.

Don't get me wrong, a lot of the time engagement between government national security organisations and average Canadians, in the form of outreach or information sessions, goes well. I am a fan of this type of exchange. In the end, however, CSIS and the RCMP are tasked with identifying, investigating, and, if necessary, arresting and prosecuting individuals and groups bent on sowing death and destruction. If this happens at the expense of good community relations, so be it. The two are not mutually exclusive but protecting Canadians trumps tea and cookies.

Another aspect of this that warrants more insight is the role played by the chief human source, Mubin Shaikh. In keeping with good intelligence practices, the identities of human sources are kept to a very small coterie in order to protect these same sources. Although I was aware that we had a highly placed agent in the group, and knew his handler at CSIS, I only learned who he was at the trial when he was compelled to give testimony.

Over the last few years Mubin Shaikh and I have become friends. He is busy on the lecture circuit and is a regular trainer of US forces on terrorism. He has done well, but at some personal expense.

Shaikh was excoriated and ostracised by many among Muslim communities in Canada for his role as a traitor, as he spied on fellow believers on behalf of the state in exchange for money. He told me in a conversation in 2020[41] that he himself had experimented with Islamist extremism, seeing the Taliban, for example, as "Islamic heroes," but had seen "the light" after studying in Syria post 9/11. He told me that he was a childhood friend of Momin Khawaja, was shocked at what his friend later got involved in, and realised he could help the Canadian government identify extremists: he actually called CSIS to offer assistance. According to Shaikh, he successfully infiltrated the Toronto 18 on November 25, 2005, and became privy to their plans to launch an attack. He explained that he acted out of altruism and wanting to "do the right thing": his appreciation for Canada increased after 9/11 and his studies in Syria.

Shaikh noted that when his identity became public and the Muslim community realised he had worked as an undercover agent it was as if a "bomb had gone off." He feels that many people, including "regular Canadians," were in denial that something of this nature could happen here. Muslims in particular, perhaps feeling under siege since 9/11, accused him of entrapping members of the Toronto 18. He believes that this view functions as a default position among some within the Muslim communities whenever an undercover operative is involved. He is convinced that they are not aware of the fact that evidence for covert criminal acts requires covert sources, and those sources are not limited to Muslims.

Despite the passage of time, and the fact that some members of the community have told Shaikh that they now realise there was indeed a terrorist plot, there is still a level of bitterness toward him. Some people have written him off and refuse to speak to him.

Shaikh also told me that the fact that nothing happened was at first seen as an indication that the plot was not serious. This is of course perverse, as the goal of counterterrorism is to stop attacks from happening, not pick up the pieces later. Incredulity about terrorists "storming Parliament" would later be seen to be real in the Michael Zehaf-Bibeau attack in October 2014. Shaikh added that he would rather have people criticise him for his role in stopping an attack than have to talk about the effects of one that was executed, resulting in deaths and injuries. He did describe the trial process as akin to being "under the microscope."

That CSIS was able to penetrate this terrorist cell is a tremendous achievement. That Shaikh agreed to go to the RCMP and act as agent—and to later testify in court—was an added bonus: not many CSIS sources do this, preferring to remain anonymous. That he stepped up for Canada and Canadians is a testimony to his character. All in all, his contribution was a major part of a very successful counterterrorism investigation by both CSIS and the RCMP (independently of course). To my mind he is a Canadian hero.

The Toronto 18 investigation was brilliant, my own bias aside. One CSIS contact told me that it felt like a redemption after the tragedy of Air India. CSIS was able to place human sources next to targets, get court appointed intercept warrants, and carry out physical surveillance. As my contact told me, this was one instance when everything was in synch" at both the regional and HQ levels: this was not always the case. The case also illustrated how CSIS and the RCMP can work together on cases of this nature. The Mounties were brought in early, intelligence was disclosed, and the RCMP launched its independent evidence-gathering efforts. When all was said and done no one died, no one got hurt, and terrorists were foiled. That is how it is supposed to work.

More recently, members of the Toronto 18 who received prison sentences have been in the news:

- Ontario's the Law Society Tribunal deemed Saad Gaya "presently of good character" thereby allowing him to become a licensed lawyer in March 2022. It was noted, however, that he had a "high hurdle" to overcome to prove the body's faith in him[42];
- Shareef Abdelhaleem, dubbed a "principal architect" of the plan, was denied full parole in September 2022[43];
- Zakarias Amara was denied parole in May 2021 despite his claims that he was "non-violent"[44].

Project Samossa

The next major plot that was disrupted by Canadian security intelligence and law enforcement agencies was one hatched in Ottawa in 2010, known in the RCMP as Project Samossa. This was a plan to attack (probably) a ceremony for deceased Canadian soldiers who had fought in Afghanistan in late 2010.

Three individuals were accused of planning the act and arrested in August 2010. The ringleader, Hiva Alizadeh, pleaded guilty in September 2014 to explosives possession and was subsequently sentenced to twenty-four years in prison. He had earlier traveled to Pakistan for terrorist training. The presiding judge noted that Alizadeh had a "radical Islamist jihadist ideology." Alizadeh's number two, a radiologist named Misbahuddin Ahmed, was found guilty on two of three charges and sentenced to twelve years in prison. Interestingly, the third cell member, a doctor named Khurram Sher famous for his Canadian Idol 'moon walk' video (he 'danced' to the tune of Canadian pop star Avril Lavigne's "Complicated"), was absolved despite the court's finding that he held jihadist sympathies.

There was a fourth conspirator as well. Awso Peshdary was also arrested in August 2010 but saw the charges dropped almost immediately. He will return later on in his role as a facilitator for Canadians seeking to join Islamic State (ISIS). This of course raises some nasty issues on how long individuals continue to hold jihadist views.

Sher proved to be an interesting wild card. Although he was acquitted, he shattered the image that many have about Islamist extremists—that they are all poor, or disadvantaged, or marginalised or uneducated. He was the ultimate exception to all of this. A pathologist in at the St. Thomas Elgin General Hospital in Ontario—just south of where I grew up—he had moved with his wife and three children and seemed to have become a success story. He had travelled to Pakistan with an aid group to assist with earthquake victims and was part of a Montreal mosque's food distribution network. Although acquitted, Sher lost his job, his family, and his reputation.

The Canadian security community received incredibly useful assistance in this investigation from domestic partners which shall remain nameless. All in all, this was a well-managed investigation (in which I played a very small part) and ended well for the government.

The Via Rail Plot

In 2013, Canadian authorities thwarted two serious Islamist terrorist plots, although one later took a bizarre twist. The first was a plan to derail a VIA passenger train in the Niagara Peninsula corridor as it traveled from New York to Toronto. Both plots involved stereotypes of who becomes a terrorist and why, and both ended in convictions, although one was later overturned in what I can only call a travesty of justice.

The VIA rail plot was called Project Smooth by the RCMP. On April 22, 2013 the Mounties charged a Tunisian student studying in Quebec, Chiheb Esseghaier, and a Toronto resident, Raed Jaser. This was one of the more bizarre cases I was involved in. And it also was seen inaccurately by many as a case involving a person with mental illness. But first the facts.

The two had conjured up an AQ-linked plot to carry out an act of terrorism and had been receiving help from an AQ member in Iran, where Esseghaier was said to have received training. Esseghaier was also believed to have had contact with someone outside Canada known as "the responsible one." who suggested that Esseghaier engage a cook to serve up poisoned food at a military base in Canada or the US.

While both co-conspirators were described by others as "devout Muslims" it was Esseghaier's faith that caused rifts with colleagues at a high-tech research facility south of Montreal. His hardline religious views were described as "troubling," as he even ripped down a poster for Canadaian charity the United Way in which women were pictured. His Facebook page allegedly showed an AQ flag—not the most subtle of approaches!

But it was Esseghaier's performance in court that had many scratching their heads. He said in open court that he did not recognise the authority of the Canadian Criminal Code as it was not based on the Quran and asked the court to judge his actions based on the Muslim holy book. During the trial he remained silent but did submit a statement after the closing arguments offering religious "advice" to the jury.

For his part, Jaser came to Canada with his parents in 1993 and was later convicted of fraud (for which he was pardoned). His religious views also raised alarms—a local imam says Jaser had talked about the necessity to "wage war against non-Muslims". Even his father was worried. Another religious leader actually called the RCMP when he noticed Jaser attempting to influence young Muslims with extremist material. Jaser allegedly once said he would like to get a sniper rifle to assassinate Canadian leaders. In March 2015 both were found guilty—Esseghaier on all five charges and Jaser on three of four.

Then things got interesting.

In August 2019, the Ontario Court of Appeal ordered a fresh trial for the men on grounds that the jury that heard the case was chosen "incorrectly," a highly technical matter that only legal experts understood. The Crown argued that granting a new trial would constitute a "miscarriage of justice."[45]

When I read this my heart sank. My first thoughts were, "here we go again." Just as in the Victoria Canada Day plot (see next section) it seemed that a terrorist case that had been brilliantly investigated and mitigated was going to suffer from an inability in Canada to prosecute these kinds of cases. The negative effect on the men and women who labour to stop terrorism should not be discounted. If thousands of hours and dollars are dedicated to stop attacks and the end result is an acquittal, it stands to reason that some practitioners would ask themselves, why bother?

In the end, however, all was well. In October 2020 the Canadian Supreme Court ruled that the "highly technical error" in the jury selection process did not in fact "cause any harm" to a fair trial process.[46] The convictions would stand.

Phew!

What I found interesting about this case was the knee-jerk reaction on the part of many in Canada that Esseghaier's courtroom shenanigans were indicative of mental illness. I beg to differ, although I must be careful here as I am neither a psychiatrist nor a psychologist. He demonstrated quite clearly that, rather than the ravings of a madman, his actions were completely consistent with someone who is deeply radicalised. His unorthodox Islamic views were textbook misconceptions common to most Islamist terrorists. His rejection of democracy and Western society is in keeping with a world view that history ended in the 7th century when Islam was dominant in parts of the world and that "true" Muslims must brook no compromise with the "heathens." His behaviour at all turns belied his radicalism, not mental illness.

The Canada Day Plot

Of all the cases I worked on, this one is both the most satisfying and the most frustrating. Very professional investigative techniques were deployed to prevent a mass casualty attack on the West Coast of Canada and a jury found the plotters guilty (two thumbs up). But, a judge later ruled that the terrorists had been entrapped by the RCMP and threw out the guilty verdicts (two thumbs down). We went from the height of victory to the abyss of defeat.

I am not an impartial observer in this instance. Not only did I work on the case while at CSIS, but I also testified for the Crown in court and contributed (a little) to the eventual guilty finding by a jury. My views have not changed in the intervening years, and I still maintain that the trial judge erred in her findings (as did a later appeals court in BC). The facts that we do know are as follows.

On Canada Day (July 1) 2013, the British Columbia division of the RCMP ('E' Division) arrested two people in Abbotsford, a city one hour east of Vancouver, and charged them with a plot to commit an act of terrorism. John Nuttall and Amanda Korody, both converts to Islam, were accused of preparing three pressure-cooker bombs on the grounds of the British Columbia Legislature in Victoria, timed to explode at 2 p.m., when the site would be crowded with Canadians celebrating the national holiday. It is worth underscoring interesting that Nuttall and Korody's attack method was similar to that used by the Al Qaeda-inspired Tsarnaev brothers at the Boston Marathon in April 2013.

The couple came from different backgrounds. Nuttall was a heroin addict receiving social assistance; Korody led a privileged life as the daughter of a dentist in St. Catharines, Ontario. They both converted to Islam and had been asked to leave a mosque in Surrey, BC for exhibiting "odd" religious behaviour. Nuttall was angry at what he called the Canadian military's 'mistreatment' of Muslims abroad, possibly a reference to the Canadian military mission in Afghanistan. He often used terms like kaffir ("unbeliever"), mushrik ("one who practices idolatry"), shaheed ("martyr") and jihad. They styled themselves as "Al Qaeda Canada" (as did the Toronto 18).

The case began in early 2013. Once it became clear that the two were serious about carrying out an act of violence, the RCMP was advised. The Mounties elected to run an officer as a "facilitator" for the pair, a fellow Muslim who was present both to make sure that the plot was unsuccessful and to see how far the couple would go. The officer offered on many occasions for Nuttall and Korody to back off: they did not.

In the end, the terrorists made several pressure-cooker bombs—inert of course, but they did not know that—and joined their facilitator in a hotel room to await the catastrophic results of their act. When nothing transpired, they were apprehended, charged, and sent to trial. On June 2, 2015, a jury found them guilty on several counts of conspiracy to commit terrorism.

This was a textbook police investigation. The RCMP controlled the operation from start to finish. There was never any danger to the Canadian public. All in all, a great job.

Until the case went to appeal. On July 29, 2016, Madam Justice Bruce ruled that the couple had been entrapped and that there had been an "abuse of process." She threw out the convictions, a decision to which the BC Appeals Court agreed in December 2018.[47]

This decision, in my opinion, was a travesty of justice. A couple of terrorists who sought to kill and maim as many innocent Canadians as they could got off because Canadian security authorities did their job. They were not entrapped: they were monitored and investigated to ensure nothing happened.

They both engaged in classic Islamist extremist rhetoric on multiple occasions and were bent on punishing Canadians collectively for our perceived aggression against Islam. These two were indeed terrorists, not random Canadians caught up by an overenthusiastic RCMP which was painted by some as the agency behind their radicalisation.

Imagine an alternate storyline. Assume that the RCMP decided that Nuttall and Korody posed no real threat and declined to follow them. Left to their own devices, the two either got lucky and planned an act by themselves or got in touch with a facilitator who was not an RCMP agent but rather a real jihadi who saw two wannabes who needed a little help. So instead of a foiled plot we had a real one and Canadians died. A very different outcome, no?

I believe that the decision to overturn the jury's verdict underscores a fundamental misunderstanding of terrorist motivation, individual capacity to carry out terrorist acts, and the methodology employed by security intelligence and law enforcement agencies to interdict terrorism. Such agencies try to determine intent and capability and yet have to tread carefully to prevent the person(s) of interest from detecting investigations.

That Nuttall and Korody had intent was never an issue. They sought to cause mass carnage all in the "name of Islam." On the matter of capability, the judge erred in concluding that the two were hapless characters. Terrorism does not require a person to be a genius to succeed. Thanks to the internet anyone, and I mean anyone, can build a bomb. Had the RCMP not intervened it is possible, if not probable, that Nuttall and Korody would have found a way to construct a device and we would all be talking about the Canada Day 2013 massacre in Victoria.

I also believe that many saw the pair sympathetically. Pictures showed Nuttall laying his head on Korody's shoulder as if he were a child. How could anyone see these two as terrorists? It was all an RCMP scam!

There are many who disagree with me on this point and they are of course entitled to their views. In the end, this case illustrates, once again, that CSIS and the RCMP are damned if they do and damned if they don't. When they stop an attack, they are accused of overreach, racism or entrapment. When they don't, they are accused of incompetence. Which one is it to be?

An RCMP contact of mine, not surprisingly, was also unhappy with the overturning of the decision. What do we do in cases where someone clearly wants to carry out an act of terrorism, but the time frame is ill-defined? Do we wait? What if we aren't watching on the day of decision? In his view this was a successful disruption: nothing happened. Can we do things better so that future cases are not thrown out on entrapment allegations? Absolutely, but there is no doubt that Nuttall and Korody posed a threat. The investigations were legitimate and justified. A terrorist attack was averted and those that wanted to cause mass carnage are now free thanks to a legal technicality.

It gets worse.

In August 2022 Nuttall and Korody announced that they are launching a lawsuit against members of the RCMP's investigating team for the "travesty of justice" perpetrated against them, claiming "serious harm, including imprisonment, emotional distress, psychiatric injuries and damage to their reputations"[48].

Only in Canada, eh!

Post-2013 Attacks

There have also been at least five successful attacks since 2013. The first were two in 2014 that occurred just two days apart: the October 20 killing of a Canadian soldier in Quebec by Martin Couture-Rouleau, a convert who had apparently wanted to fight in Syria, and the October 22 killing of reservist Corporal Nathan Cirillo at the National War Memorial in Ottawa by Michael Zehaf-Bibeau and his subsequent unsuccessful attack on Parliament. In 2016 there was an attack on a Canadian Armed Forces recruiting centre in Toronto, and then in 2017 an attack on a police officer and civilians in Edmonton, and an attack in a Toronto-area hardware store.

I have elected to treat this era differently for several reasons. One, I was not at CSIS after October 2013 and hence do not have the same memories or access to intelligence on these cases and therefore must rely solely on open-source information. Two, my contacts who worked at CSIS were not involved in these cases either, thus removing a perspective that proved so useful in the previously discussed attacks and plots. Finally, it was only after 2013 that attacks were successful. I do not, by the way, associate my absence from the frontlines with this change in the terrorism environment: it is clearly coincidental.

In the absence of available intelligence to add to an understanding of these acts, the following descriptions will be general in nature, based on news accounts. My analysis will also be general in nature.

October 2014 Attacks

Although these are two completely unrelated attacks, I have elected to discuss them in the same section for two primary reasons. Their virtual simultaneity—Couture-Rouleau's act took place on October 20, 2014, and Zehaf-Bibeau's two days later—is a remarkable coincidence. Secondly, both terrorists were frustrated foreign fighters who chose to strike within Canada: this aspect will be looked at in some detail later.

Martin Couture-Rouleau

On October 20, 2014, a car hit two members of the Canadian Armed Forces while they were walking in a parking lot southeast of Montreal. One victim, Warrant Officer Patrice Vincent, died of his injuries. The driver, Martin Couture-Rouleau, fled the scene but was engaged by police and shot dead when he ran at officers with a knife.

Couture-Rouleau was yet another convert to Islam obsessed with ISIS, such that he had been listed as a "high-risk traveler," someone keen to leave Canada to join a terrorist group and engage in violent jihad. He had tried to do so in July 2014, resulting in the seizure of his passport. Efforts were made by several parties to steer Couture-Rouleau from his ideology and it appeared to be working as late as two weeks before his attack.

After his conversion to Islam he frequented violent jihadi websites and expressed a desire to die a martyr. Like Nuttall, he was critical of members of the Canadian military, who he said were pawns of the Canadian foreign policy establishment. He was also angry at Canada's role in bombing ISIS.

Michael Zehaf-Bibeau

On October 22, 2014, Michael Zehaf-Bibeau left a homeless shelter in Ottawa and walked to the Canadian National War Memorial, metres from Parliament Hill. Armed, he fatally shot Nathan Cirillo, an unarmed Canadian reservist performing honour guard duties at the cenotaph. Jumping in a car, he drove across the street, abandoned the vehicle and tried to breach the Centre Block of Parliament where he was killed by the sergeant at arms. Despite drug abuse issues he had appeared to live a normal early part of his life (though, he too was a convert to Islam).

Like Couture-Rouleau, Zehaf-Bibeau's passport had been seized on suspicion he had jihadist sympathies. He once attended a mosque in Burnaby, BC where he was described as "rude" and angry at the mosque's open-door policy, which he believed allowed too many non-Muslims to visit.

After the attack, a video was found in which he was critical of Canada's foreign policy and claimed that his upcoming attack was a form of retaliation for the situation in Afghanistan. He noted that targeting soldiers in Canada was justified so as to show Canadians they were not safe in their own country. In summary, he issued threats that attacks like his would continue until Canada and its allies ceased to occupy Muslim countries and kill its citizens.

Interestingly, ISIS lionised both Couture-Rouleau and Zehaf-Bibeau online for their actions, and later took credit for inspiring the attacks. There is another significant similarity: both featured in Issue number 5 of ISIS's *Dabiq* magazine.

Aside from the temporal juxtaposition of the attacks, both Couture-Rouleau and Zehaf-Bibeau targeted uniformed members of the Canadian military in their attacks. This strategy is not all at surprising. Islamist terrorists often cite foreign military campaigns as justification for their acts. It is also noteworthy, as already mentioned, that both had initially sought to fight abroad but were prevented from doing so. The issue of these so-called "foreign fighters" will be picked up later in this chapter.

Interestingly, Zehaf-Bibeau's act eclipsed that of Couture-Rouleau by a large margin: the latter became almost a footnote in Canadian media reporting. The reasons for this should be of no surprise. Zehaf-Bibeau's attack began at the national cenotaph in the very heart of Ottawa. The memorial is well known and attracts tens of thousands of Canadians every

November 11 for Remembrance Day, when the sacrifices of the men and women who died in wars in which Canada had participated over the decades are commemorated. It is an iconic monument.

His subsequent move involved an even more iconic structure: Canada's Parliament building, and more specifically, the Centre Block. This magnificent sandstone building draws hundreds of thousands, if not millions, of Canadian and international tourists to Ottawa every year. It would be hard to find a Canadian who was not familiar with it. In addition, then Prime Minister Harper was meeting with his caucus metres away from where Zehaf-Bibeau breached the building. A contact confided to me that the PM was not happy with his security services for letting a terrorist get that close to him!

In essence, Zehaf-Bibeau was striking at the heart of Canadian democracy. Jihadis hate democracy and everything it stands for. His attack was an attempt to frighten all Canadians and mock the very system of government we have held for 156 years.

Ottawa went into lockdown for eight hours after the attack. There were rumours of a second gunman who was headed toward the Rideau Centre, a major shopping mall a few hundred metres from the cenotaph, and of snipers on the roofs of neighbouring buildings. Neither proved to be accurate but the police had to be certain.

I was not in Ottawa the day of the attack. Ironically, given that I had specialised in Islamist terrorism for a decade and a half at CSIS, and then with Public Safety Canada, I was giving a lecture on radicalisation to a crowd of officers from the Toronto Police Service together with a CSIS colleague when news of the shooting came in. I then moved to a pre-arranged presentation for officers from OPP-PATS, a service I was to join in May 2015 when I retired from the federal government. I recall receiving updates on my cellphone from a colleague at Public Safety Canada as I was driven from one venue to the other. It was not until late in the evening of 22 October that I returned to Ottawa.

The following day I left very early in the morning for my office at Public Safety in the core of the city and stopped at the cenotaph. There were already thousands of flower bouquets laid to honour Corporal Nathan Cirillo, such that it was hard to see the pavement. I spent a few minutes there thinking of this soldier and how he had been killed by a Canadian jihadi, and I apologised silently for our collective inability to prevent his death.

Zehaf-Bibeau may or may not have been on the intelligence radar in October 2014. He certainly had come up in conjunction with others of interest. Was he missed? Was he assessed to not pose a threat? Did he fall through the cracks? I have no idea, although I cannot help but think that CSIS and the RCMP must have done an internal review to see what they knew (and didn't know) and why.

The underlying conundrum for security intelligence and law enforcement agencies in cases like these is that we are faced with individuals bent on leaving Canada to join a terrorist group. We cannot acquiesce to this desire as we have an international responsibility to not let Canadians kill and main people abroad, as will be discussed in the next major section. Hence, when we are aware of such intentions, we stop these wannabe jihadis by seizing their passports.

Unfortunately, in many cases there is not enough information—by which I mean evidence—to lay charges. These frustrated terrorists are thus left to roam free and may or may not be subject to continuing investigations. Both of these cases appear to be instances of radicalized individuals thinking "if I can't engage in terrorism over there, I might as well do it here." Authorities are thus left in a "damned if we do and damned if we don't" situation again. Anyone who maintains that there is an easy solution to any of this is ignorant of the challenges faced by security and intelligence agencies.

One last note. I referred earlier to the belief that a second shooter had left the scene and headed toward the Rideau Centre, a Cadillac Fairview property. I interviewed the former head of national security at Cadillac Fairview in November 2020. He walked me through the challenge of working out what was happening when there was inconsistent and contradictory information coming in as the attack unfolded. There never was a second shooter: the belief that there was one may have been spurred by some who saw the second honour guard flee in the general direction of the Rideau Centre. This underscores once again the difficulty in separating fact from fiction in the midst of an ongoing crisis.

May 2016 Stabbing in Toronto

Many assume that terrorists must be mentally ill. After all, according to this reasoning, how could a normal person choose such a career? The levels of violence and depravity associated with terrorist groups, especially ISIS, lead most to see terrorists as being "not like us."

As I demonstrated in *The Threat from Within*, however, the opposite is true. The vast majority of Islamist terrorists do not show any identifiable signs of mental illness and are "like us" (in a sense, of course—most people do not choose to behead their enemies). And yet, this stereotype continues. Still, it is possible that on rare occasions the presence of a mental disability may cloud our understanding of an event.

An attack that occurred on March 14, 2016, at a Canadian Armed Forces recruitment centre in north Toronto was carried out by one Ayanle Hassan Ali. He slashed two soldiers with a knife, wounding both slightly, and tried to stab another three before he was overpowered. At Ali's trial, the judge agreed that he was motivated by his "radical religious and ideological beliefs" but acquitted him on account of his "mental disorder."[49]

Ali's lawyer observed that two psychiatrists, one for the defence and one for the Crown, both noted that "his relationship with Islam became tied up with his schizophrenia and he sat alone in his room for years hearing voices . . . and conflating in his mind the voices that he was hearing and the symptoms of the schizophrenia with messages of radical Islam," and condemned the Crown for bringing terrorism charges in the first place. Nader Hasan, one of Ali's lawyers, stated "They had someone who they thought looked the part of the terrorist, when in reality they had someone who committed a terrible, terrible act, who was mentally ill, and they should have proceeded in that fashion rather than over-reaching for terrorism."

For its part, the Crown criticised the judge's ruling that Ali's offences could not be seen as terrorism under the Criminal Code as it is not possible for one person to constitute a "terrorist group."[50]

I am not qualified to rule on a psychiatrist's finding of a mental disorder, but I do think that the judge demonstrated profound ignorance of Canada's terrorism laws. Nowhere in the section of the Criminal Code that deals with terrorism does it talk about a "terrorist group" as a necessary condition for an act of terrorism. This ruling—mental illness aside—demonstrates, once again, the Canadian judicial system's woeful lack of understanding of the reality of terrorism, a point I will return to in the penultimate chapter.

A Near Miss: The Aaron Driver Case[51]

On August 10, 2016, the RCMP headquarters in Ottawa got a call from a Federal Bureau of Investigation agent who said that the Bureau had come across an ISIS-inspired martyrdom vide on the Internet in which a man in a black balaclava had a chilling message: "Oh Canada, you received many warnings. You were told many times what will become of those who fight against the Islamic State. There is a fire burning in the chest of every Muslim, and this fire can be cooled only by the spilling of your blood. . . . (ISIS leader Abu Bakr al-Baghdadi) has called for jihad in the land of the crusaders. I am responding to that call."

Not surprisingly, the RCMP took this threat seriously and tried to identify the man in the video. Within a few hours they had a match: Aaron Driver, a 24-year-old convert to Islam who resided with a sister in Strathroy, Ontario. The Mounties went to investigate and at 4 p.m. that same day Driver exited his house into a waiting cab and exploded a small device in the back seat. The bomb lightly injured the cab driver, and Driver was killed by RCMP fire when he left the car.

All in all, this was a success story. The case speaks highly of the relationships that Canadian security intelligence and law enforcement agencies have with their international counterparts, on this occasion the FBI. No one was killed other than the terrorist. A possible much larger attack was thwarted, as Driver had two bombs in his knapsack. According to my RCMP contact the whole incident played out over just twenty-four hours. In other words, despite the lack of time and advanced warning the outcome was a good one.

On the other hand, we got lucky. It was not as if Driver was an unknown quantity. He was already on a peace bond for, among other things, praising ISIS atrocities, talking to like-minded extremists online, and justifying the 2014 Parliament Hill attack by Michael Zehaf-Bibeau by saying, "they weren't attacks on civilians or attacks on women and children. They were attacks on uniformed soldiers and members of the government."

And yet he was probably deemed a low risk to commit an act of terrorism. The system—any system—is far from foolproof. There is no algorithm or template to determine with any degree of certainty who poses a real threat and who is nothing more than a talker. The RCMP probably had higher priorities at the time.

This incident raises all kinds of questions about the usefulness of peace bonds for terrorists and points out that the good guys sometimes get their "man" at the last possible hour. Aaron Driver was not an anomaly. Other Canadians, as we have seen, and as we shall see below, act alone in what they see as part of a greater terrorist cause. To date, thank God, the casualty rate in Canada has been low.

June 2017 Toronto Attempted Stabbing: Rehab Dughmosh

Occasionally, you come across an incident that really makes you say to yourself, "Huh?" In June 2017, a woman draped in an ISIS banner went into a Canadian Tire hardware, lunged at employees with a golf club—yes, a golf club—and a butcher's knife, while yelling "this is for ISIS." She also had a bow and arrow to be used as a weapon. Thankfully, no one was seriously hurt, and the employees were able to subdue the woman until police arrived.

The woman in question is named Rehab Dughmosh and her story is one which demonstrates the tenacity and dedication of radicalised Islamist extremists. She is also another case in Canada of an individual whose initial goal was to engage in violent jihad abroad, but whose intentions turned to Canada when that desire was foiled. Dughmosh left Canada and attempted to travel to Syria in April 2016 to join ISIS, but Turkish officials denied her entry. The RCMP had learned of her plans from her brother and appear to have alerted the Turkish authorities. Upon her return to Canada, she was interviewed by the RCMP and denied she wanted to hook up with ISIS, claiming she was only going to visit family in Syria. After a second interview a few months later the RCMP did not see enough evidence to lay charges and closed the file.

Note that this is not atypical in counterterrorism cases. The vast majority of cases I was privy to never got to the point where they needed to be disclosed to the RCMP for possible criminal investigation and charges. The bar is a high one in Canadian courts and terrorism is a difficult crime to prove beyond a reasonable doubt. To my mind this is because of the need to demonstrate that an act of violence was planned or executed (or both) for motives that speak to political, ideological, or religious drivers. All these are psychological constructs that may not be obvious: hence the tendency to use other parts of the criminal code (murder, attempted murder, conspiracy, etc.) which can more easily lead to successful prosecutions. This is, after all, the end goal: the Crown does not go to court to lose.

But back to Dughmosh. The following details come from a very good report penned by a reporter with the Toronto Star in January 2019,[52] during the trial for this wannabe jihadi. A year after her unsuccessful foray to join ISIS, Dughmosh began to make homemade weapons, including a child's shovel she made into "claws," thirty-six cardboard handles studded with screws, and seventy-six nine-inch straws stiffened with paper and tape with screws on the ends. These may not strike the reader as very lethal, but they can nevertheless inflict serious injury if used properly (or the person wielding them gets lucky). She also purchased a compound bow and two arrows from the same Canadian Tire store in which she later carried out her attack.

According to the statement of facts, on June 3, 2017, Dughmosh packed three bags with her homemade weapons as well as thirty-one barbecue skewers, scissors, and a hammer. No one can say she wasn't prepared! She also packed two arrows and hid the bow and an eight-inch butcher's knife under her clothing.

As she was leaving to carry out her attack, she ran into her husband in the lobby. He asked her what was in the bags, and after looking inside one, he took them away from her. But he was unaware of the bow and the knife she had concealed in her clothing. Dughmosh then walked to the Canadian Tire store about five minutes away.

After failing to purchase more arrows, Dughmosh walked around the store, picking up various tools, such as a hammer, heavy wrenches, and pliers. She then picked up a golf club and put everything into a shopping cart. Next, she proceeded to take out the bow and a black and white homemade ISIS banner which she tied around her head. With the golf club in one hand and the bow in the shopping cart, she pushed the cart toward three Canadian Tire employees and two customers.

Dughmosh "charged towards them, swinging the golf club and repeatedly shouting "Allahu Akhbar" and 'This is for ISIS.'" Following a brief struggle—and after she had pulled out the knife and slashed it toward an employee—the employees were able to disarm her. Incredibly, while the Canadian Tire staff waited for police to arrive, one of the employees recorded a discussion between him and Dughmosh. When asked why she was trying to kill the employees, Dughmosh openly admitted that she wanted "revenge for Muslims. . . . Stop killing Muslims in Syria and Iraq. . . . You are killing ISIS, I'm from ISIS, ISIS is Muslims, stop killing Muslims."

Following her arrest, Dughmosh told RCMP investigators she had started supporting ISIS in 2014 and viewed ISIS propaganda videos online. She said she pledged bayat ("allegiance") to ISIS leader Abu Bakr Al-Baghdadi, although it does not appear that anyone with the terrorist group actually received her pledge.

Dughmosh told investigators that she decided to do the attack on a Saturday because there would be many people around, and she went to the Canadian Tire store because that was where she had bought materials for her homemade weapons. She did not want to kill people, she said, only hurt them and make them feel fear, and was disappointed that she failed to actually hurt anyone but added that the important thing was to try.

At her trial, in which she elected to represent herself, Dughmosh barely spoke. She appeared to refuse to recognise the authority of the court. We saw this same attitude in the Esseghaier case earlier. In February 2019, Dughmosh was found guilty of four terrorism charges and sentenced to seven years in prison.[53] The presiding judge noted that her "mental illness" (likely schizophrenia) was a factor in handing down such a light penalty.

October 2017 Edmonton Vehicular Attack

The Canadian Football League (CFL) is a poor country cousin of the much better known (and promoted) National Football League (NFL). Nevertheless, the CFL is older than the NFL and its championship game—known as the Grey Cup—dates back to 1909, well before the Super Bowl. Still, it is a small league and one that is constantly on the brink of folding.

In Western Canada, especially in the provinces of Manitoba, Saskatchewan, and Alberta, however, the CFL is big news and remains very popular with fans. Tens of thousands attend games, making them a big deal around town. Is it that surprising, then, that such a venue would attract a terrorist?

On October 30, 2017, a car veered into an Edmonton Police officer directing traffic outside an Edmonton Eskimos game at Commonwealth Stadium, sending him several metres into the air. The driver exited the vehicle and proceeded to stab the officer several times. Luckily, the officer was wearing body armour and was able to defend himself, resulting in non–life-threatening injuries.

The man, who we later learned was named Abdulahi Hasan Sharif, fled the scene and later drove a rented truck down a major Edmonton street, deliberately hitting four pedestrians (again, no one was killed). The truck he was driving was rammed by a police cruiser and flipped on its side. Sharif was tasered and arrested. An ISIS flag was found on the dashboard of the truck.

Claiming to have been captured in his native Somalia by the AQ-linked Al Shabaab, Sharif was also known to be spouting extremist Islamist rhetoric as early as 2015, but the investigation into him was discontinued. A person who used to work construction with Sharif told police that the latter held "genocidal beliefs" and had "major issues with polytheists." He also alleged that Sharif talked about hating Shia Muslims and expressed support for ISIS.[54]

Mental illness was again cited as a contributing factor in the case, but in October 2019 a jury found him guilty on five counts of attempted murder as well as dangerous driving and criminal flight causing bodily harm. A judge sentenced him to twenty-eight years in prison.[55] He was not charged with terrorism.

This case raises some interesting questions. Foremost, why no terrorism charges? Perhaps the difficulty in proving ideological, political, or religious motivation played a role. If attempted murder is easier to establish, why take a chance with proving terrorism?

Furthermore, again we have a case that had come to the attention of law enforcement agencies and was dropped. I am convinced that this illustrates two fundamental issues: one, an incomplete understanding of radicalisation and violence; and two, an overworked police force. If charges are not immediately obvious and other cases are seen as a higher priority, such cases as this one can fall off the agenda. In this instance, Sharif did indeed pose a significant threat and it is only through good fortune that no one died.

2019 Young Offender Plot

Kingston, Ontario, is a city located on Lake Ontario just as it empties into the St. Lawrence River. It is both a university town, home to Queens University, one of the country's oldest post-secondary institutions, and a slew of prisons. It is also the city most associated with Scottish-born Sir John A. Macdonald, Canada's first prime minister.

What it is not known for is terrorism.

Yet following a tip from the FBI, the RCMP raided a Kingston house in January 2019 and arrested two people, including a 17-year-old man. Given his age at the time, under Canadian law he is classified as a young offender and cannot be publicly named. He was communicating with what he thought was an ISIS sympathiser in Virginia. The man on the other end was actually an FBI agent. The Kingston man forwarded instructions on how to build a pressure-cooker bomb and urged his online interlocutor to plant it in a public place, such as a bar, to kill infidels in an attack that would help ISIS.

In July 2020, the young offender pleaded guilty to several charges, among which were facilitating terrorism and planning to detonate an explosive device underneath a police or military vehicle (there's that military angle again!).[56] The case demonstrated extremely close cooperation among the FBI, the RCMP, CBSA, the OPP and the Financial Transactions and Reports Analysis Centre of Canada (FINTRAC). The RCMP even deployed a surveillance aircraft over Kingston for some time.

Canadians Who Planned or Committed Attacks Abroad

Some Canadian Islamist terrorists elect to carry out attacks outside Canada. The reasons for this are undoubtedly complex. Whatever the drivers, having Canadian citizens kill and injure people in other lands reflects poorly on Canadian law enforcement and security intelligence agencies which have failed to interdict them. The list is short, but still too long. One is too many.

Momin Khawaja

A saying that may be heard in intelligence circles is, "Never be caught in the office on a Friday after 4 p.m." That seems to be the time when something is guaranteed to come in just as you are getting ready for your weekend. I cannot count how many times when I was at CSE in the 1980s and 1990s, usually anxious to get on the road to see my fiancée in Toronto (and later my wife and kids at home), that my boss would come to me and say "Phil, we need you look at this right now."

That "right now" would often turn into several hours as the information might need to be translated, then written up in a report, sent to a client who was waiting for it—probably just as impatiently—and then the need to hang around for feedback or questions. Then, and only then, was I released.

Something very much like this transpired on a Friday afternoon in February 2004. I was heading out of the CSIS parking lot when I saw a colleague from our Ottawa Region office heading in the opposite direction. I asked her what was up, and she cryptically replied that the British Security

Service had advised that a bunch of Islamist extremists they had been following, who they believed were planning a terrorist attack in the UK, had just been joined at an Internet café by a Canadian. During this man's February 2004 trip to the UK, he met with the UK terrorist cell headed by Omar Khyam. The cell was being monitored by UK security agencies, who witnessed the man show his friends a device he had created.

And this was not just any Canadian. This was a Canadian with a device that could suppress cellphone signals within a specific radius. This was a Canadian with a desire to help out an operational cell in the UK. This was a Canadian who was born and raised in Ottawa. This was a Canadian named Momin Khawaja.

Suffice to say that no one got a lot of down time that weekend, especially the regional investigators who had to work at figuring out who Momin Khawaja was and what he was up to. Plans were made to get a federal court intercept warrant as soon as possible and to arrange for physical surveillance once Khawaja returned home (which he did shortly afterwards). This case called for a full-court press and everything possible was done to gain as much intelligence as possible on this Canadian co-conspirator.

In the end Khawaja, a contract computer programmer with the Canadian Department of Foreign Affairs, Trade and Development. was accused of having been part of a plot designed by a UK cell to detonate a 600 kg bomb in London. He and his British co-conspirators were arrested in separate operations led by Canadian and UK authorities in March 2004.

Khawaja's trial did not start until 2008. In October a court found him guilty on five of seven terrorism-related charges and in March 2009 he was sentenced to ten and a half years in prison. The defence countered that Khawaja wanted only to fight allied soldiers in Afghanistan and was unaware of the plans by his UK buddies. Both the defence and the Crown appealed. In December 2010 the Ontario Court of Appeal increased Khawaja's sentence to life (mostly because he showed no signs of giving up his extremist beliefs). He remains at the Special Handling Unit, a federal super-max prison in Sainte-Anne-des-Plaines, Quebec.

I was in a pub in The Hague, Netherlands, with a colleague from the UK Foreign and Commonwealth Office when my Blackberry (remember them?) went off and informed me of the new life sentence handed to Khawaja. I actually yelled out loud, attracting the stares of the other patrons, before settling down. It was a great moment to be a Canadian involved in counterterrorism.

So, who was Momin Khawaja?

He had gone to Pakistan several times, supposedly to visit family, although intelligence in both Canada and the UK believe that the real reason was to train in a terrorist camp (including alongside two members of the cell that carried out the 2007 London tube attacks). Once back in Canada he began to obsess about the fate of Muslims in Chechnya and Palestine and the killing of innocent Muslim women and children. Together with a few friends he would play paintball in out of the way spots for which they used the most Canadian of codewords: hockey.

What would lead Khawaja down this path? That is not certain. He was raised in Orleans, a suburb east of downtown Ottawa, and a popular choice for civil servants. Khawaja and his siblings led a good life. His father had a PhD in social sciences and Khawaja certainly appeared to be fully integrated into Canadian society: he himself told a reporter that his childhood had been normal.

During his second year at Algonquin College in Ottawa he began to change, growing a beard, praying five times a day, and, most importantly, obsessing about the plight of Muslims around the world. He believed that the US was a sponsor of terrorism and an oppressor of Muslims.

The rest, as they say, is history.

I met Khawaja on a few occasions. It is my opinion that he still held to the same opinions and the same ideology that landed him in jail. While I last saw him several years ago it still worries me that he may get out one day. It is my assessment that, once released, an individual like Khawaja would need to be watched to determine what level of threat he still poses to Canadian society. This issue will be examined in some detail in the last chapter.

What is also interesting about the Khawaja case is the speed with which it went from initial investigation to arrest (that it took four years to come to trial is a different matter altogether). This was rare in my experience during my years at CSIS. Most investigations lasted many months or years as more intelligence was gathered to see how serious the individual was about engaging in terrorism as well as how many others were involved. Sharing intelligence with law enforcement is another consideration that must be carefully worked out. That Khawaja was seized so quickly speaks to both the nature of what he was involved in and its immediacy. The alacrity with which this was all done speaks highly to the capabilities of the agencies involved. As one contact told me this case was an "enormous success."

July 2012 Bulgarian Bus Attack

You will recall from the introduction that I chose not to include the Hizballah terrorist group in this book. Not that this Lebanese organisation is not worthy of discussion when the subject concerns terrorism. Yet, the group's activities in Canada appear to centre on financing and "creative" shipments.

An attack in Bulgaria is the one exception to this decision since it involved a Canadian. On July 18, 2012, a tour bus parked at the airport in the southeastern city of Burgas was bombed, killing five Israeli tourists and a Bulgarian driver. A dual Lebanese-French citizen, Mohamed Hassan El-Husseini, was also killed as he placed an explosive-laden backpack in the bus's luggage compartment.

Two accomplices, Meliad Farah, 39, an Australian of Lebanese origin, and Hassan El Hajj Hassan, 32, a Canadian of Lebanese origin, fled the scene. In September 2020, a Bulgarian court found both men guilty of providing logistical support to terrorism. They were tried in absentia.[57]

The attack was seen as linked to Hizballah. I recall hearing of the blast while I was at CSIS, and learning that a Canadian passport document had been discovered at the scene. The incident surprised me then and continues to do so now. That a Canadian would travel to Bulgaria of all places to carry out a terrorist attack still strikes me as odd.

January 2013 In Amenas Attack

I hail from London . . . Ontario, not the UK. It is a mid-size Canadian city (population 180,000 when I grew up, now over 400,000). Nothing much happens in London. It is a mixture of offices and industry, much of the latter rusted out in the typical North American downturn in that sector of the economy. My late mother, who was born in Montreal, never liked London. She called it boring. For me it was ok, although I left in 1983 to work at CSE in Ottawa and have lived in that region ever since. In all honesty, I was ready for life in the "big city," even if it was in a government town where many complained that the pace of life was slow. There is a pedestrian street called Sparks Street in the centre of Ottawa, one block from Parliament Hill and lined with government offices, and many have joked that you could fire a cannon right down the middle of the road at 4 p.m. on a weekday and all weekend and never hit anybody!

Yet a few years back my hometown made international news for a connection to terrorism. In January 2013, news broke that two Canadians were part of a terrorist attack in which at least forty workers were killed at a gas plant in southeastern Algeria. In April of that year the RCMP identified the bodies of two London, Ontario natives—Xristos Katsiroubas and Ali Medlej. The pair had left Canada for Morocco in 2011 after which they were allegedly trained in Mali by by Mokhtar Belmokhtar, a North African terrorist linked to Al Qaeda in the Islamic Maghreb. Interestingly, the pair was originally a trio: a third Londoner, Aaron Yoon, was arrested in Mauritania and spent two years in jail on terrorism charges before returning to Canada in 2013.

The attack unfolded early in the morning on January 16. Gunmen affiliated with AQ crashed their vehicles through the gates of the complex and quickly rounded up many of the employees. Hostages noted that one of "the Canadians" was clearly in charge: that was apparently Katsiroubas. The terrorists made demands—the freeing of AQ prisoners held by Algeria and the US and provision of a plane to fly them to Mali.

Soon after, helicopter gunships began to fire on the complex, wounding some of the terrorists. Eventually they decided to make a run for it and were all killed, either in the getaway trucks or in the complex.

Those who suffer from terrorism are not only the victims and their families. The parents of one of the three (whom I have met, but who shall remain anonymous here) were at a complete loss to understand and accept that their son had become a terrorist. This couple had nothing to do with their son's path to terrorism, unlike cases where terrorism is a family affair (hello Khadrs!). I cannot imagine how one comes to terms with the fact that one's child aspires to take, or takes, the lives of others in a violent way and as part of a terrorist group. It has to be tough, although some parents try to make the best of a very difficult situation—see the section below on Damian Clairmont.

I do not recall any investigation into these three before the attack in 2013, although that may be a memory lapse on my part. The fact that they made their plans from London may have played a role in their ability to stay under the radar. London is equidistant from both Toronto and Windsor, where CSIS has regional offices. Canada is a big place and Ontario itself is not small either. Manning investigations in a land this size is a challenge.

There is another aspect to this affair that needs to be mentioned. Most Canadians, I imagine, would assume that terrorism is something that originates in, or targets, our larger cities: Montreal, Vancouver, Toronto, and Ottawa. As this story illustrates, however, that is not true. Canadians can radicalise to violence anywhere, not just in major urban settings. Part of this is explained by the ubiquity of online fora, which today reaches most parts of the country, albeit sometimes at slower speeds (Internet at the vacation cottage in central Ontario is maddeningly snail-paced!).

I was part of investigations that looked at Canadians in very small places, even hamlets. I recall a location in northern New Brunswick that I needed an atlas to find! It is not always about large concentrations of individuals in the same urban setting. It is about enough like-minded people who share a cause. This is what happened in "boring London."

We will see other examples in the paragraphs that follow which will underscore this phenomenon in Canada. Towns and villages far from the mainstream will feature time and again. And yet, whenever these cases hit the media there is inevitably always the same expression of surprise: "How could this happen in ____?" (Fill in the blank with some out-of-the-way locale.)

Hence my contention that a security service with somewhere between 3,000 and 4,000 employees, a small minority of which are actual investigators, cannot do it all. Individuals and plots will fall through the cracks. Not all successful attacks are intelligence "mistakes" à la Air India. Some are all but unstoppable. That is the reality of counterterrorism work, in Canada and elsewhere. Our men and women at the ramparts are good but they are not perfect.

Salman Ashrafi

For reasons that may not seem obvious at first, Calgary, Alberta, became a hotbed for Islamist extremism in the early 2010s. Several residents left Canada to join ISIS or other terrorist groups. Most of them have died or are believed to be dead.

In one case, however, a young Calgarian left Canada and died in a suicide bombing in Iraq. Some might immediately conclude that the man in question was born on the wrong side of the tracks or had nothing to live for. He was probably uneducated, underemployed and may have had mental issues. Sound familiar? I bet it does. And it is all completely wrong.

Salman Ashrafi was doing well for himself. Very well. He held jobs with energy firms such as Talisman and Exxon and was a University of

Lethbridge graduate. One acquaintance said of him: "On the one hand, he was an extremely kind and gentle person, but he also had a very black and white view of the world. A kind of simplistic view of the world."[58]

In 2012 he left Calgary and ended up in Iraq, where in November 2013 he was part of a double suicide attack that left forty-six Iraqis dead. ISIS released footage claiming him as its own. As for his family, they have had a difficult time accepting the manner in which his life ended.

Mahad Dhore and the "Canadian Somalis"

Beginning in the mid-2000s we in the security intelligence community began to hear rumours of a few Somali Canadians in the Greater Toronto Area who were believed to have left Canada to join the terrorist group Al Shabaab in Somalia. The timing was likely not a coincidence. Al Shabaab had arisen in the wake of the demise of the Islamic Courts Union (ICU), which was defeated in part by an invading Ethiopian force.

One of those who travelled was named Mahad Ali Dhore, who is thought to have left Canada in 2009 to enlist in Al Shabaab. In April 2013 he is alleged to have died in a suicide attack in Mogadishu that killed twenty-nine people and injured at least fifty-eight. Al Shabaab claimed responsibility on Twitter, writing that "there is no safe haven for apostates in Mogadishu!"[59]

Dhore immigrated to Canada when he was nine and later attended York University in northern Toronto. Prior to his travel, he had told family that he was planning to live with an aunt in Kenya, where there is a large Somali diaspora in that country's northeast, near the two countries' shared border. He lied.

Another Somali Canadian, Muhammad Elmi Ibrahim, who went by the name "Canlish", had a eulogy posted on an extremist website noting he "died in battle" sometime in 2010. In addition, two Canadian Somali females travelled to join Al Shabaab in 2011.

Back in Canada, Mohamed Hersi was tried in a Brampton court in May 2014 and charged with attempting to leave Canada to join Al Shabaab in 2011, an act he described as "God's will". On May 30, 2014, Hersi was convicted of attempting to participate in terrorist activity: two months later he was sentenced to ten years in prison.

The large Somali diaspora which has made Canada home has for the most part fled a disastrous situation in their homeland: famine, war, and terrorism. The trauma that all this has engendered cannot be dismissed. And yet citing that as the main driver for why a handful have elected to leave their adopted country ignores the uncomfortable fact that only a handful has done so. This underscores again that the decision to join a terrorist group and take part in an act of extreme violence is a highly personal one.

An interesting role was played by a Toronto resident, Fadumo Jama, who became known as "Mama Shabaab." She ran a safe house that catered to Westerners who travelled to Somalia to join the terrorist group. The Toronto Star's Michelle Shephard wrote a long report on her back in 2012.[60]

July 2016 Café Attack in Bangladesh

A few years ago, I found myself in Dhaka, the Bangladeshi capital, on a business trip to share some findings about online radicalisation with local officials, including the Rapid Action Battalion (RAB), who are that country's counterterrorism SWAT team. One evening a colleague and I went for coffee at the Holey Artisan Café. While there was a sleepy security guard outside, all looked ok. We had a coffee and pastry and left.

The café was anything but ok on July 1, 2016. A terrorist cell inspired by ISIS took twenty hostages and slaughtered them all: nine Italians, seven Japanese, two Bangladeshis, one American and one Indian citizen.[61]

The ringleader was Tamim Chowdhury of Windsor, Ontario. Two months after the massacre at the café he and two other terrorists were killed by the RAB in a raid on a house near Dhaka. In keeping with a trend, we have already seen, Chowdhury was no marginalized Canadian: he had a chemistry degree from the University of Windsor. Despite his good prospects, he left Canada in 2013 destined for Syria. He died as a terrorist but not before he was believed to have also been involved in an attack on a prayer gathering in which four Bangladeshis, including two police officers, were killed on July 7 of that same year.[62]

Canadians Who Joined Terrorist Groups Abroad

According to the Canadian government, on several occasions in recent years, "hundreds" of Canadians have left our fair land to join terrorist groups abroad. These individuals are generally known as "(Western) foreign fighters" or "foreign terrorist fighters" (FTFs). The Canadian number, to the best of my knowledge, has never been categorised by time periods or geographic locale. The best we know is that a third are believed to be dead, a third are back in Canada, and a third are still outside the country.

Unlike the cases presented above, the ones featured here are not tied to a specific act of terrorism. Many have already featured in previous publications and the purpose of this section is to establish basic facts and conclude with an analysis of what should be done with those who either have somehow succeeded in returning to Canada or who are sitting in limbo abroad seeking to come home.

For a more detailed look at why these individuals opt to become part of terrorist groups, the reader is encouraged to look at my book, *Western Foreign Fighters: The Threat to Homeland and International Security*. I will not repeat the arguments made in that book here.

For ease of presentation, I will discuss these cases geographically, starting with the West Coast of Canada and moving eastward. Most provinces of the country have seen at least one, and more often several, Canadians leave to join a terrorist group. The nation's three territories (Yukon, Northwest Territories, and Nunavut) and four Atlantic provinces (New Brunswick, Nova Scotia, Prince Edward Island, and Newfoundland) are exceptions (as is the prairie province of Saskatchewan). This should be of no surprise. The territories are sparsely populated and have very small Muslim populations. Similarly, Canada's easternmost provinces have never figured prominently in national security files when it comes to terrorism, likely for the same reasons.

I will also include those who sought to leave Canada for terrorist activity but who were prevented from doing so by law enforcement or border officials. I will return to this issue in the analysis section.

Note that this section is not exhaustive in nature. There are some cases I am unable to include as they are not part of the public record. During my time at CSIS we encountered many individuals who spoke of a desire to leave the country to join a terrorist group. Some did, although most did not. Not all these cases are of common knowledge and I am constrained in commenting on them for reasons I hope are clear.

One contact did state that the security community was slow to move from an emphasis on Afghanistan and Pakistan to what was happening in Iraq and Syria with the advent of ISIS. There had been so much occurring on the ground with the former AQ network and there was so much to investigate. This speaks to the resource issue I will return to in the penultimate chapter.

British Columbia (BC)

We have already discussed the Nuttall-Korody terrorism plot which was fully formed within BC. There has been at least one resident who has elected to leave the province to join ISIS in Iraq/Syria.

Hasibullah Yusufzai

On January 21, 2014, Hasibullah Yusufzai, an Afghan Canadian, left Burnaby, BC, to join unspecified Islamist fighters in Syria.[63] He was later charged with leaving Canada for the purpose of committing murder "for the benefit of, at the direction of or in association with a terrorist group." An Interpol "red notice" was also issued in which photos portrayed a young man who had undergone a significant physical transformation. Yusufzai posted on Facebook that he wished to move to a Muslim country and denounced "so-called Muslims" in Canada. In another Facebook post he wrote: "It would be better to live in an Islamic country ruled by a 'tyrant' than to live in a darul kufar ("land of disbelief"). . . . No one can fully practice their religion in Canada. Can one talk about jihad in a khutbah (sermon)? They can but soon they will be reported to the authorities by the so-called Muslims."[64]

I recall an interesting aspect of this case. After his disappearance from BC, Yusufzai's family discovered a letter he had written in which he asked for forgiveness and requested that his credit card debts be repaid. These are two important signs of violent radicalisation and mobilisation. Aspiring jihadis are told that if they die in battle with financial debts their martyrdom is null and void. Furthermore, by begging contrition for their sins they prepare for entry into Jannah (paradise) where they will be in a position to vouch for seventy of their relatives who will also gain eternal life upon their deaths. These issues are discussed at greater length in my first book, *The Threat from Within*.

Alberta

Alberta has posed an interesting challenge from a security intelligence perspective. The security community learned that one mosque-musallah ("Islamic prayer centre") in particular in downtown Calgary, known as the 8th and 8th mosque,[65] had a disproportionate number of members who elected to leave Canada to engage in terrorism. Several of the cases presented below were individuals who frequented that mosque.

Damian Clairmont

In early 2014 Canadian media reported that a young man from Calgary, Damian Clairmont, another convert to Islam, had died fighting jihad in Syria. His beliefs were in part betrayed when he told a friend interested in joining the Canadian military that they were killing Muslims. He was particularly focused on what was happening in Syria and sought to "help" the situation.

Clairmont had issues with depression—he was diagnosed as having bipolar disorder—and he dropped out of high school and attempted suicide. He then converted to Islam and appeared to put his life back together. His family noted that it helped to calm him down. According to his mother, "he did seem to find some peace. Then he changed." He moved into a boarding house, and became very secretive, very angry and very political."

Clairmont told his mother in late 2012 that he wanted to go to Egypt to study. He actually flew to Turkey and then crossed the border into Syria. According to some reports he joined Jabhat al-Nusra ("al-Nusra Front"), an Al Qaeda affiliate in Syria. It was reported in the media that Clairmont died in Syria either in late 2013 or early 2014.

I had long chats with Clairmont's mother following my retirement from CSIS in 2015 and she featured in a podcast with me in June 2020.[66] She is critical of the Canadian government and its agencies for failing to stop her son from leaving to engage in terrorism.

The Gordon Brothers

Gregory and Collin Gordon were converts to Islam who lived in an apartment building in the early 2010s that also housed Damian Clairmont and Salman Ashrafi. In other words, they too were part of the "Calgary cluster" that was occupying a lot of the security intelligence community's time in the Alberta city. Community members claimed that the pair disappeared in late 2012: Collin posted pro-ISIS propaganda on Facebook. Like so many other Canadian jihadis, they were from a stable family and were well educated.[67] An ISIS member tweeted in December 2014 that the brothers had been killed in Dabiq, Syria.

Farah Shirdon

Canadians and others first met Calgary resident Farah Shirdon via two online videos in 2014. In the first he is seen to burn his Canadian passport and boast "We are coming for you!" He later told a VICE News reporter that Canada and the US were run by tawaghit ("tyrants"), that he wanted to be a martyr, and that he would engage in beheadings and the enslavement of women and children.

In September 2017, the US Central Command (CENTCOM) announced that Shirdon had been killed in July 2015 in an airstrike in Mosul.[68]

Sohail Qureshi

Born in England, Sohail Qureshi moved to Canada as a child, first to Saskatchewan, then to Calgary at age fifteen. While studying computer science at university, he tired of what he calls a "thug life" and turned to the Internet. "That's when I looked to religion and went deep and deep and deep," he says of a faith that was so literal and extreme that it was all-consuming. His parents were alarmed by his transformation into a fledgling jihadi and sought the advice of a local imam, who told their son to "stand down."[69]

Qureshi did not listen. After graduating in 2006, he left Calgary for Pakistan with the goal of joining the Taliban. He claimed he did nothing of a terrorist nature while there and was escorted back to Canada by the RCMP. He says he is a changed man. "This whole story is not just about going from a terrorist to a citizen, but going from someone who's a prisoner to someone who's free."[70]

Hussein Borhot

In July 2020 the RCMP charged Hussein Sobhe Borhot with "participation in activity of a terrorist group and commission of an offence for a terrorist group."[71] The Calgary man travelled to Syria from May 2013 to June 2014 to join ISIS, which trained him and had him participate in kidnappings. The charges were laid after a seven-year investigation, underlining how difficult it is to amass evidence in these cases.

Sayfildin Tahir Sharif

In January 2011 the RCMP arrested Edmonton resident Tahir Sharif after an investigation carried out jointly with the FBI into a Tunisian foreign fighter–facilitation network. They accused Tahir Sharif of conspiracy to commit terrorism and of participation in several suicide attacks in Iraq in 2009 in which US soldiers were killed. The US government wanted him extradited to the US: an Edmonton judge ruled in 2012 that there was indeed enough evidence to do so and he was extradited on January 23, 2015.

Like other Canadian jihadis he wanted to die a martyr and was angry at the US invasion of Iraq.

Abdullahi Ahmed Abdullahi

On October 17, 2022 a US court sentenced Edmonton resident Abdullahi Ahmed Abdullahi to 20 years in prison for assisting at least six Canadians and Americans in joining ISIS in 2013 and 2014[i]. The court found that Abdullahi had funded acts of violence, including kidnapping. Abdullahi's cousins in Minnesota and Edmonton were among those he aided to travel to Iraq and Syria.

Canadian authorities had arrested Abdullahi in 2017 and extradited him to the US in 2019. The ISIS terrorist had robbed a jewelry store in 2014 to help him raise funds for the terrorist group. He pleaded guilty to material support for terrorism in 2021.

This case leads to an interesting question: why did Canada send him to the US when his crimes (robbery, terrorist financing) occurred in Canada? Yes, he was apparently a resident of San Diego, but is it not incumbent on judicial officials to see him punished here? Or did officials think the US had a stronger interest (given the Minnesota link)? Perhaps they realised that the US deals with terrorist offences more seriously than we do: it is highly unlikely he would have been handed a 20-year jail term in Canada (recall that several of the Toronto 18 members were released after having been found guilty of conspiracy to commit a terrorist act on the basis of 'time served' in pre-trial detention).

Manitoba
The Winnipeg Trio

In all my time at CSIS, the following case stood out for the central province of Manitoba.

In 2010 it was learned that three students from the University of Manitoba, Maiwand Yar, Ferid Imam, and Muhanad Al Farekh, had dropped out of school suddenly three years previously and gone to Pakistan.

The RCMP put out a "wanted poster" in conjunction with conspiracy to participate in terrorist activities in what is known as Project Darken. The RCMP stated that the trio had gone to Pakistan for terrorist training: US intelligence maintains Imam became a weapons instructor at a training camp in Peshawar and provided support for a 2009 plot to plant a bomb in the New York subway system.

In April 2015 Al Farekh, who is a US citizen, was captured in Pakistan and flown to the United States for trial, where he was charged with supporting terrorism.[72] Yar and Imam are believed to have been killed. The sudden, and on the surface unexplained, disappearance from Winnipeg led to much angst within the local Muslim community. To them, the trio appeared well integrated, were involved in community events, and no one had reported any signs of radicalization.

The reaction of the community is understandable but inaccurate. We detected a radicalisation process, which should suggest that others could as well. Interestingly, there were actually four individuals, not three, that were planning to leave together. The fourth elected not to, and to this day it is not clear why he made the decision to stay. What this illustrates is that radicalisation is a very personal and idiosyncratic process. Expecting predictability is a fool's errand.

Ontario
Andre Poulin

There are times when you come across a terrorism case and ask yourself "WTF"? This is one.

Andre Poulin was born in Timmins, Ontario, a small town in the northern part of the province perhaps best known internationally as the birthplace of the singer Shania Twain. It was here that he converted to Islam after a few run-ins with the local constabulary.

Poulin left behind a detailed video on his life — ISIS put it online in July 2014. Here are excerpts from that video:

> I was like any other Canadian. I watched hockey. I went to the cottage in the summertime. . . . I liked outdoors, I liked sports. . . . but Allah guided me from the darkness of kufr [the infidel] to the light of iman [faith]. . . . Before I came to Syria, I had money, I had family, I had good friends. . . . I always had family to support me. . . . It's not like I was some kind of social outcast. . . . Life in Canada was good. . . . But at the end of the day it's still Dar al-Kufr [the world

of the infidel]. . . . They [Canadians] use these taxes in their war on Islam. . . . [Contributions to the Islamic State] are obligatory on us. . . . There is no better land than Sham [Syria/Levant], so come and join.

Poulin also encouraged others to travel to Syria to help fight jihad and was killed for his efforts.

The narrator of that video lionised the dead terrorist.

John Maguire

Speaking of small towns, meet John Maguire, born in Kemptville—thirty minutes south of the nation's capital. Like Poulin he was featured in an ISIS video released in late 2014 in which he too alluded to his "normal" upbringing (hockey!). He then claimed that the October 2014 attacks in Canada that killed Nathan Cirillo and Patrice Vincent were linked to Canada's role in the "war against Muslim people." Maguire urged Muslims living in Canada to travel to live under the ISIS Caliphate, or follow Martin Couture-Rouleau's lead and carry out attacks in Canada.

An ISIS Twitter account announced in early 2015 that Maguire had been killed near a town on the Syrian border with Turkey.

Mohamed El Shaer

Mohamed El Shaer of Windsor, Ontario, was arrested by the RCMP in June 2014 on a terrorism peace bond, a provision introduced in the Canadian Criminal Code that makes it easier for police to arrest people who haven't committed a crime. Just days after serving several months in jail for committing passport fraud (he falsified information on a Canadian Citizenship and Immigration form he filled out in Turkey), El Shaer was quickly rearrested as the RCMP suspected he would leave the country to join a terrorist group.[73]

It is important to point out that El Shaer was not charged with terrorism at the time, despite his pattern of travel to the Middle East that was indeed special in nature. His lawyer argued no current travel restrictions were necessary for his client in light of his track record.

A few years back I had travelled to Windsor to participate in a session on violent radicalisation organised by, and at the invitation of, local Muslim youth. I was accompanied by officials from Public Safety Canada's Citizen Engagement branch and an RCMP outreach officer. My role was to talk about my research on radicalisation and what signs communities could detect to identify individuals heading down the path to violent extremism.

As soon as I had finished my talk, a young man stood up and took me to task. He accused me of Islamophobia and exaggerating the threat to Canada from terrorism. He added that no one in Windsor would share the ideology I had just demonstrated and that he was insulted that a government of Canada delegation would come to his city to talk about a non-existent problem. And he wouldn't shut up.

His remarks led to an argument with the others in attendance, none of whom appreciated his outburst or the rudeness with which he had greeted their guests. At one point the scene almost led to fisticuffs. One member of the community apologised to me privately saying "he's our local extremist." As a seasoned intelligence analyst specialising in homegrown radicalisation, I had noticed that.

That man, I later learned, was Mohammed El Shaer.

What I found significant in this affair was the audacity and brashness with which an apparently radicalised person acted in a public forum. There is a myth that the greatest threat to our security comes from so-called sleeper cells. In reality, the vast majority of those who radicalise to violence betray their ideology openly, and those who go on to commit terrorist acts actually tell people in their ambit about their plans in what is called "leakage." It is as if the commitment to their ideology is so thorough that the radicals cannot help but share it with everyone. In addition, these individuals do not care about being detected by law enforcement (recall that an RCMP officer was in attendance that evening). This may sound counterintuitive: wouldn't those engaged in activity that may be seen as criminal tend to hide their ideas? On the contrary, this bizarre behaviour happens more often than not whether it is in a mosque, a classroom, or any other venue. The reasons why they are so brazen are not well understood. It may come down to a belief that their path is the true one and that whether or not they succeed is in the hands of another. We have actually seen foreign fighters tweet their conviction that "Allah blinded" authorities to their plans, allowing them to get to Iraq or Syria to join Islamic State.

In addition, violent radicals also "out" themselves in order to identify others for recruitment potential. And this appeared to be what happened in Windsor that night. Despite massive opposition to what he was saying and doing (kudos to the community for standing up to him), I noticed two young men who seemed enthralled by his words. I have no idea what eventually happened to these two—in fact I spent the better part of an hour trying to convince one that choosing El Shaer's path was not a wise move—but it would not be hard to imagine them getting hooked.

In my experience, El Shaer's behaviour is typical. I did not know much about him when I witnessed his performance that evening in Windsor, but what I saw evoked for me the mindset of an Islamist extremist. Luckily, for communities as well as for security intelligence and law enforcement agencies, such individuals conveniently help us identify them through their words and actions.

It is worth noting that other countries have detected extremist infiltration into community events. An Australian youth worker noted in December 2020 that de-radicalisation programs in his country were "deeply flawed" and routinely infiltrated by members of Islamist extremist gangs posing as either volunteers or participants. He went on to say:

> When you get a whole heap of young people who are at risk and you're bringing them together for intervention programs and community barbecues, what you're doing is telling these predators where to find them. You're doing them a favour and then it's like shooting fish in a barrel. What they do is, the senior recruiters, they . . . send young Arab guys into these outreach activities to mingle with the other young people and make out like they are volunteers and that they're somehow part of the service. All they're really doing is fishing out the most vulnerable kids. That's when the older guys come down and start indoctrinating them and preaching to them. It's incredibly difficult to police. Instead of shutting them out, de-radicalisation programs are opening new pathways for these guys and inviting them back in. They're using the system against itself and we're losing a lot of young kids to them.

Vilyam (William) Plotnikov

Russian security forces claimed to have killed Vilyam (William) Plotnikov, a Russian emigrant to Canada, in an engagement in the Dagestan region in July 2012, where the Canadian had joined an Islamist extremist militia. According to other sources, Plotnikov may have known Tamerlan Tsarnaev, one of two brothers accused of setting off the Boston Marathon bombs in April 2013. Another convert to Islam in 2009, Plotnikov left a note for his parents saying he had gone to France for Ramadan but ended up in Moscow where Russian officials claim he became a terrorist, traveling to Dagestan to be with other Islamist extremists. Plotnikov referred to himself as a terrorist and expressed confidence that Allah would bless his plans to attack the West. After his death a jihadist site called Plotnikov a martyr.

The Jabarah Brothers

The details provided here are derived from *The Martyr's Oath*, Stewart Bell's excellent book on a case of homegrown Al Qaeda terrorism in Canada. His account is comprehensive and well written and, for the purposes of our discussion, does not need to be expanded upon.[74]

Abdul Rahman and Mohammed Mansour Jabarah were born in Kuwait and survived the the Iraqi occupation of their country in 1990 and 1991. They and their parents traveled to Canada three years later, settling in St. Catharines, Ontario. Based on initial observations the pair seemed to fit in well in their new home.

They traveled back to Kuwait in the summers and on one such trip were introduced to Sulayaman Abu Ghaith, a cleric who taught that jihad was a duty for all Muslim men. Abu Ghaith himself had fought in Bosnia and parlayed his battlefield experiences and propaganda videos to convince the boys that they too should act. Abu Ghaith was in effect an AQ recruiter.

Even while back in Canada their desire for jihad only increased. The Russian war in Chechnya appeared to inspire them. They spent a lot of time on jihadi websites and watched extremist videos. In 2000, they travelled to Afghanistan where they received terrorist training and where Mohammed pledged allegiance to Al Qaeda leader Usama Bin Laden.

AQ sent Mohammed to Singapore to carry out a number of bomb attacks against Western targets. Luckily those plots were foiled, forcing Mohammed to flee. He was eventually arrested in Oman in 2002, flown back to Canada and handed over to the US. He was tried, convicted, and sentenced to life in prison. As of 2014 he is in a maximum-security prison in Colorado.

As for Abdelrahman, he went to Saudi Arabia in May 2002, joined an extremist group, and was later accused by Saudi authorities of preparing attacks. He was killed in July 2003 by security forces in a shootout.

Kevin Mohammed

Twenty-seven-year-old Kevin Omar Mohamed was arrested in 2016 on the campus of the University of Waterloo when he was found in possession of a number of items, including a hunting knife, a large quantity of money, and handwritten notes based on information found on AQ websites for how to plan and carry out an attack. Mohamed pleaded guilty to supporting AQ-linked Jabhat al-Nusra and was sentenced to four and a half years behind bars, but was released in 2019 upon receiving credit for time served.

Mohamed was rearrested on July 8, 2020 for breaching his probation order by having a device capable of accessing the internet and placed on a peace bond meant to "mitigate the risk of him committing a terrorist-related offence." His lawyer claimed that he had travelled to Syria to "help Syrians with the humanitarian crisis," but that "he recognised that he went about it the wrong way."[75]

Awso Peshdary

Awso Peshdary is an interesting case. He was arrested in August 2010 in conjunction with Project Samossa detailed above. After a brief stay in custody, he was released, only to be rearrested and charged with domestic assault against his wife. Released yet again, he rejoined Ottawa society.[76]

Peshdary does not seem to appreciate his freedom. He was arrested a third time in February 2015 and charged with "recruiting, financing and facilitating terrorism." He is alleged to have been very close to John Maguire (see above) and was seen as a "star recruiter" of Ottawa wannabe jihadis, including the Larmond twins (see below).

As of the time of writing, Peshdary's case is still before the courts and a verdict may hang on the defence's allegations that a federal court warrant granted to CSIS to monitor his communications in the early 2010s was obtained "illegally."[77]

The Larmond Brothers

Carlos and Ashton Larmond, proteges of Awso Peshdary and converts to Islam, were keen to join ISIS. In January 2015, Carlos was arrested in Montreal while trying to travel to Syria and sentenced to seven years in prison: Ashton was arrested in Ottawa at the same time and received a 17-year sentence. While incarcerated in pretrial custody, Carlos was busy trying to radicalise other inmates, telling some that if they did not convert to Islam their families on the outside would be killed by ISIS. For his part, Ashton stated that he wanted to "slit a soldier's throat" and noted, in reference to a 2014 attack at the Lindt Café in Sydney, Australia, "You take the head off one of them, then you're in control."[78]

Carlos is already out of prison and living in a halfway house in Calgary.

In November 2020 he was granted overnight privileges after telling the Parole Board of Canada that he wanted to visit a ski resort with his girlfriend. Officials believed his commitment to Islamist terrorism has been discontinued.[79]

Ikar Mao and Haleema Mustafa

In December 2019, a southern Ontario man who once stood trial in Turkey for having alleged links to ISIS was arrested. The RCMP charged Ikar Mao of Guelph with one count each of participating in the activities of a terrorist group and of leaving Canada to take part in terrorist group activity. The following August, his wife, Haleema Mustafa, was also arrested and charged with the same offences.[80] This marked the second time a husband-and-wife team in Canada had jointly engaged in believed terrorist activity, the first being John Nuttall and Amanda Korody.

Shehroze Chaudhry

The case of Shehroze Chaudhry, also known as Abu Huzayfah Al-Kanadi, is an odd one. He claimed to have travelled to join ISIS and to have become an enforcer who killed civilians. After returning to Canada, he featured in a ten-part *New York Times* podcast series written by Rukmini Callimachi entitled Caliphate. In those recordings he said he had witnessed shootings, beheadings, and crucifixions and that he himself shot civilians who had been blindfolded in the back of the head. To say that the news was shocking would be an understatement.

Then, in September 2020, the RCMP arrested Chaudhry and charged him—but not with terrorism offences.[81] He was accused of having made the whole story up and now faces terrorism hoax charges. Many people have been embarrassed for having swallowed Chaudhry's tales.

I met with Callimachi in May 2018 at her office in New York, where I was presenting at the annual conference of the American Psychological Association. We spoke for hours about counterterrorism and CSIS and my views on terrorism. She elected not to include any of my thoughts in her podcast, which was of course her prerogative.

What this shows me, however, is that everyone who listened to Chaudhry committed the cardinal sin that all intelligence personnel are wary of: a failure to corroborate information. Sources lie all the time for reasons that vary widely. The CIA, of all agencies, put much stake in the source Curveball who reported on Iraqi President Saddam Hussein's ties to AQ: look where that ended up. That Chaudhry's allegations were not backed up using independent sources should be a lesson to all: intelligence agents, journalists, and the rest of us.

Ali Dirie

As far as I can tell, Ali Dirie is the only person in Canadian history to have been convicted of a terrorist offence (he was a member of the Toronto 18), serve prison time, and be released only to leave Canada to join a terrorist group overseas. His role in the Toronto 18 was to acquire guns in the US along with Mohamed Yassin: the two went on to be tried and convicted. While in jail Dirie continued to contact Toronto 18 leader Fahim Ahmad, advising him on the upcoming plans to carry out bomb attacks.

For this he was reconvicted of terrorism, and in the end he served a total of seven years. Upon his release in 2011 he obtained a passport and left for Syria where he allegedly died while fighting with Jabhat Al Nusra.

Dirie's story raises important questions about the tenacity and staying power of radicalization. Despite his long prison term he was not rehabilitated and did not abandon the ideology of Islamist terrorism.

Quebec
Said Namouh

Returning to the theme of small town terrorism we come to Said Namouh, a resident of Maskinongé, northeast of Montreal. He was arrested in September 2007 and charged with conspiracy to cause death in an attack to occur outside of Canada (later charges included participating in the activities of a terrorist group, facilitating terrorist activity, and committing an offence on behalf of a terrorist group. Namouh is thought to have been a member of the Global Islamic Media Front (GIMF), an international propaganda network for Al Qaeda. He is also believed to have had ties to a cell in Austria that wanted to punish Austria and Germany for the presence of their troops in Afghanistan. That cell may have been planning a car bomb in Vienna as well as the 2008 UEFA European Football Championship in Austria and Switzerland.

A common theme reappeared with Namouh: a desire to punish the West for its actions against Islam. Namouh was convicted of four terrorism-related charges in October 2009 and sentenced to life in prison. Upon the completion of that sentence the Canadian government voiced its intention to deport him to his native Morocco, as he does not hold Canadian citizenship.

Montreal Teens

In April 2015 a Montreal couple, Sabrine Djermane and El Mahdi Jamali, were arrested while trying to travel to join ISIS. They claimed they were planning to visit Greece. The pair were charged with attempting to leave Canada to commit a terrorist act, possession of an explosive substance, and committing an act under the direction of, or for the profit of, a terrorist organization.

They were acquitted in December 2017 but placed on a peace bond which outlined several conditions: a prohibition against using social media, weekly check-ins with the RCMP, and avoiding Montreal's Assahaba mosque, which is linked to the controversial imam Adil Charkaoui. He is of note, as he was one of the famous national security certificate cases to be discussed in the penultimate chapter.[82]

What to Do with "Foreign Fighters"?

Now that we have looked at all the cases of most relevance in Canada, let's look at what all this means. The Dughmosh case discussed above is illustrates what has been labelled the "foreign fighter" problem. Thousands of Westerners travelled to Iraq and Syria in the mid-2010s to join ISIS and other terrorist groups. Many died but many were captured as well. Among the latter some were tried in Iraqi or Syrian courts and sentenced, some to death. The rest are in a variety of camps in the region and local authorities are begging their home governments to repatriate them. Most countries, Canada included, have refused, despite pressure by some lobby groups to bring them back.

In my opinion, the reluctance to have committed terrorists in our societies in understandable. No government wants to expend effort to rescue a violent extremist only to see that person go on to spread Islamist extremist ideology at home or, as in the case of Dughmosh, actually attempt to carry out an attack.

There are other considerations as well. A returned jihadi is someone who has to be monitored to determine capability and intent. This all requires resources that are already maxed out. Bringing charges is fraught with difficulties stemming from gathering evidence in a war zone. The public wants nothing to do with these fellow citizens who deliberately opted to join a terrorist group that slaughtered thousands.

Those who claim that some of these detainees no longer pose a threat owing to their renunciation of terrorist ideology are on very thin ground indeed. Who determines this and how? There are certainly no guarantees in this regard. As for de-radicalisation programs, these are largely more hopeful than effective.

A government that makes efforts to repatriate Canadian terrorists will face a serious backlash at the polls. That being said, there does not appear to be any legal obligation to do so. Canadians who "get into trouble" overseas can ask for consular assistance, but they are not immune from local legal proceedings. The government cannot refuse to allow a Canadian to return home, and there does not seem to be an appetite to rescind citizenship as in some Western nations, but it does not have to facilitate that return. Consequently, the current government will in all likelihood muddle its way through this conundrum. The Dughmosh case shows what happens in the worst possible scenario. Don't expect any prime minister to repeat any time soon Justin Trudeau's line "a Canadian is a Canadian is a Canadian" when it comes to terrorism. Then again, stranger things have happened in politics.

One of the most frequently raised objections to Canada's inaction in bringing home Canadian terrorists is the concern that either the local jurisdictions abroad do not want to legally try (or do not have the capacity to try) these individuals (for example, the non-state Kurds in northern Iraq and Syria) or their judicial systems leave a lot to be desired (for example in Iraq and Syria, with rapid trials, no effective defence, the possible use of torture, capital punishment, etc.). Aside from the reality that Canada cannot tell a sovereign state how to run its own courts and prisons, and every traveller should know the laws and penalties for contravening those laws, I find it curious why there is a lobby group within Canada pushing for repatriation. After all, there does not appear to be an analogous group backing child molesters or drug dealers languishing in similar conditions. Nonetheless, this group has had success: in late January 2023 a court ordered the Government of Canada to bring ISIS terrorists back from overseas.

Another specious argument is that by not bringing our own citizens home we risk the possibility that they will be resentful and become more radical: a few may seek to plan attacks here or elsewhere to achieve some level of revenge. Firstly, there is no data I am aware of to support this position; and secondly, what does "more radical" mean? These people were radical enough to join a heinous terrorist group, the activities of which they were fully aware (or should have been aware. ISIS and others were not shy about boasting of their depraved actions). How can they become even more radicalised?

This whole issue may become moot as Swedish authorities announced in October 2020 that some Kurdish authorities had agreed that Swedish ISIS recruits could indeed be tried in situ, in a form of international tribunal, which Sweden has been arguing for over the past few years.[83] A court of this nature would be optimal for at least two reasons: justice would be seen to be done where the crimes occurred; and witnesses would be easier to identify, obviating the need to bring terrorists and victims back to the West (or other areas of the world that fed the ISIS beast).

It is likely that some people would criticise CSIS and the RCMP from allowing Canadians to leave Canada in the first place with the intention of joining a terrorist group. The argument would go something like this: if we do not want to have terrorists plan and execute attacks on our soil, why would we allow them to do so elsewhere? Are the lives of non-Canadians not equally as precious?

In a perfect world, Canadian authorities would indeed identify and hamper travel plans of this nature. There are, however, several obstacles to this:

- It is not always clear that a given individual intends to travel for terrorist purposes.
- In many cases the information is too vague to lead to charges under the Canadian Criminal Code: as one contact told me "there was nothing we could do about it—we may not have had enough evidence to press charges and our hands were tied."
- Canadians have a Charter right to leave Canada.
- Many individuals had not crossed the security "radar" before their departure and hence left undetected. Some who have come to the attention of security intelligence and law enforcement agencies are able to evade interdiction as blanket surveillance is rarely a possibility.
- Canada's track record to date in charging and successfully

prosecuting wannabe foreign terrorist travellers is terrible. The lack of prosecutorial success may lead to a sense of apathy within the security intelligence community.

As the phenomenon of terrorist travellers is unlikely to disappear, it is incumbent on the Canadian government, the judicial system, the country's security intelligence and law enforcement agencies and even the Canadian public to do a better job in this regard. We cannot become a nation which "exports" its terrorist problem.

What About the Others "of Concern"?

It is worth pointing out that CSIS has stated publicly that it is engaged in several hundred terrorism investigations at any given time.[84] Assuming that the majority of these are tied to Islamist terrorism, as has been the case in recent history, this implies that there is a large number of people that have not been arrested or are no longer in Canada, having left the country to join a terrorist group. So, the question remains, what are these people doing?

We used to call this bunch "couch jihadis." These people are radicalised and do support the use of violence but for a variety of reasons—perhaps lack of opportunity or motive or resources—have yet to act. Given that CSIS and the RCMP do not want to spend resources on individuals who may be unlikely to do anything, what should be done in these cases? It should be stressed that there are reasonable grounds to suspect that these individuals are engaged in activity that poses a threat to national security. This suspicion is what CSIS uses, under its legislation, to launch an investigation. There are compelling reasons to not prolong investigations, however, ranging from a practical need to manage workload to the more serious requirement that the State not unreasonably subject its citizens to intrusive investigation.

This is a vexing and challenging issue. As there is also no predictive model of who will move from advocating violent extremism to engaging in violent action it is thus impossible, given the current state of knowledge and understanding, to determine who should be monitored and for how long. Obviously, if a person demonstrates a clear abandonment of violent extremism, they are no longer of immediate concern to security or law enforcement agencies. Caution must be exercised here, however, in that saying you no longer entertain extremist views does not mean you have truly abandoned them.

Getting this wrong has severe consequences. Hence a constant re-evaluation and triage is required to determine where to allot precious few resources. Agencies are subject to review to assure that they are operating within their legislative mandates.

One of the most famous examples of a triage that went badly is the case of Mohammad Sidique Khan, the ringleader of the July 7, 2005, attacks in London. Khan was on the radar of the UK security intelligence service, MI5, but was judged not essential because there was no intelligence to suggest that he was planning an act of terrorism.[85] This assessment turned out to be wrong.

It is important to emphasise that saying that MI5 failed to determine the level of threat posed by Khan is not a criticism of the abilities or capabilities of that service. MI5 has to allot its resources in accordance with the competing priorities it encounters. They cannot and surely would not want to look at everyone. They make the best decision at the time based on the best information available. In this case, an individual not believed to be an imminent threat turned out, unfortunately, to be exactly the opposite.

No one should be so smug as to suggest that the monitoring of violent extremists is easy or that deciding who poses the greatest danger is an obvious choice. Decisions are often made when exhaustive information is not available. Agencies make the best choices possible under the circumstances. It is hoped that those choices are the correct ones. There is never a guarantee, however: actions taken or not taken may not prevent a given act of terrorism from taking place.

Summary

What this chapter has demonstrated quite concretely is that when it comes to Islamist extremism, Canada has experienced a level of violence significantly lower than that of its primary Western allies: for example, the US, the UK, France, and Belgium. Two deaths in the post-9/11 period is a remarkably low number indeed.

Still, that achievement requires a better explanation. In part, Canadian Muslims have fared better than their counterparts in Europe, many of which are economically challenged and have been subjected to significant discrimination (not that either factor leads inexorably to violent radicalisation, as I pointed out in *The Threat from Within* in 2016).

Canada is also a relatively minor player on the international stage and more specifically in Muslim-dominant regions. We are not a former colonial power like France. We are not an occupier like the US in Iraq, although we did contribute troops to Afghanistan post 9/11 and to France's Operation Barkhane in the Sahel. As a result, we are not high on the "jihadi radar" for retribution.

And yet we have experienced at least five successful attacks in Canada by homegrown Islamist extremists. As well, at least four major attacks were averted thanks to good security intelligence and law enforcement operations. And then there were the four attacks carried out by Canadian jihadis abroad, in addition to the hundreds of Canadians who left to join terrorist groups elsewhere. In other words, this is a serious problem for Canada, both internally and externally.

What is most fascinating about the Canadian Islamist extremist crowd is their ordinariness. They come from all walks of life: privileged and less so; educated and uneducated; Muslim-born and converts to Islam. There is no pattern to their circumstances that can be used to "profile" them.

However, they all share the same underlying ideology. Regardless of whether they saw themselves as AQ or ISIS or Al Shabaab (and may have pledged allegiance to a group), they all hew to the same set of beliefs. It is this commonality which differentiates Islamist extremism from other types (the far right, to be discussed in the next chapter, is a dog's breakfast of causes and grievances).

This form of terrorism is seen by some as "yesterday's threat." There are constant calls to refocus security intelligence and law enforcement resources to the far right, as if Islamist extremism has disappeared. A move of this nature would be folly.

A cursory glance of the news on any given day shows that Islamist extremists around the world still commit 99 percent of all terrorist attacks. The right wing is clearly a movement of concern, in some Western nations more than others, but it pales in comparison to the jihadis on a global scale.

Canada's Islamist extremists may have been quiet during the recent past, but they are not gone. We would be wise to dedicate the necessary money and people to continue to monitor this threat.

4

Other Forms of Terrorism

WHILE ISLAMIST TERRORISM may indeed have posed the greatest public safety threat since 9/11, terrorists inspired by other ideologies have not been entirely absent. This chapter will look at a couple of successful attacks attributed to these underlying drivers.

Introduction

In this chapter I will look at what I am terming "other" forms of terrorism in Canada. Although this term conveys very little to the reader, I believe that the acts of terrorism described here are in essence a "grab bag" of causes and ideologies.

This chapter could also have been entitled "Right- and Left-Wing Terrorism." Neither term is ideal for several reasons. What do we mean by right- or left-wing? Is one's position on the ideological or political spectrum not in the eye of the beholder? What if certain acts of violence belie easy placement on an ideological or political line?

There is also a significant difference, at least to my mind, between the violent movements and acts to be covered here and those in the previous two chapters. Nationalist or ethnic terrorism is readily defined: it is tied to a specific cause or grievance linked to a specific geopolitical entity (e.g., Armenia or Iran). Similarly, all Islamist extremists and Islamist extremist groups can be reduced to essentially the same underlying motivation: a desire to impose a narrow, hateful, intolerant version of Islam on the Muslim world (and beyond, in their wildest dreams!).

Not so with the far right- and left-wing actors. The former range from white supremacists to white nationalists to neo-Nazis to conspiracy theorists. It is far from clear that there is one common driver, even if there are some commonalities (for instance, positions that are anti-immigrant, anti-Semitic and Islamophobic). The same can be said for the left-wing bunch. Within that description is found environmental activists, anarchists (though this term can also apply to right-wing actors), and social justice warriors, among others.

There are those far more specialised in, and therefore better placed to discuss, the nature of this kind of violence. Nevertheless, in a book on terrorism in Canada it would be remiss to ignore these actors as there have been at least two terrorist incidents tied to them (one each as it turns out).

That being said, there has arisen a change in the Canadian government's terminology selection when it comes to terrorism in recent years, directed largely (but not solely) at what we see as right-wing extremism. This shift has been both unnecessary and unhelpful: I will return to this issue in the next chapter.

That very last statement should raise some eyebrows. When compared to the previous two chapters, this one will be vastly shorter. Simply stated, there have been very few acts of terrorism in Canada attributed to either the right or left wing to date. There is good reason to believe that this may change in the years to come, and indeed may already be changing—a topic I will interweave in the two sections presented here.

Right-Wing Terrorism in Canada

To date, there has been one act of serious violence in Canada that can safely be described as a right-wing terrorist incident. On Sunday, January 31, 2017, at 8 p.m. in the evening, 27-year-old Alexandre Bissonnette walked into the Islamic Cultural Centre in Québec City and opened fire. When he had finished his killing spree, six people lay dead and another five had been wounded.

Bissonnette was arrested and charged, and he pleaded guilty to six counts of murder and five of attempted murder. He was sentenced in February 2019 to life in prison with no possibility of parole for forty years. In November 2020, an appeals court reduced that sentence to twenty-five years after it ruled that consecutive life sentences are "cruel and unusual":[86] another black mark on the Canadian judicial system when it comes to terrorism prosecutions.

This case presents several interesting aspects, including the possibility that it was not an example of right-wing terrorism. As my friend and colleague Benjamin Ducol, formerly lead researcher at Montreal's Center for the Prevention of Radicalization Leading to Violence (CPRLV) told the CBC, Bissonnette presented traits observed in both mass shootings and terrorism cases: "That's why it's so difficult to put Alexandre Bissonnette somewhere, because he's kind of in the middle of these two phenomena, and I think it's stuff that we are seeing much more right now."[87]

This is a very important point and demonstrates why labelling an act of serious violence as "right-wing terrorism" is problematic. A lot of this activity could just as easily be described as hate crimes, for which the Canadian Criminal Code has provisions. While there was some evidence that Bissonnette dabbled in far-right online forums, it is telling that the Crown charged him with murder, not terrorism.

To my reckoning, all terrorism is a form of hate but not all hate is a form of terrorism. Many acts of violence (assault, attempted murder, murder, etc.) can in fact be motivated by hate, but that hate is not necessarily describable as terrorism, which requires a driver that is political, ideological, or religious in nature. Furthermore, at least in Canadian law as I understand it, serious crimes can be tried using "ordinary" provisions of the Criminal Code and any tie to hate can be taken into consideration by the judge upon sentencing after conviction (interestingly, this is not the case for terrorism).

The nebulous relationship between hate and terrorism can be seen in a recent case in Canada. In February 2020, a man alleged to be an incel (involuntary celibate) killed one woman and wounded another in a Toronto erotic massage parlour. He was charged initially with first degree murder and attempted murder: those charges were changed to terrorism in May 2020.[88] He pleaded guilty to first degree murder in September 2022[89]; at the time of writing the Crown had yet to decide whether to keep pursuing the terrorism charges. Why? First degree murder already carries an automatic life sentence and nothing more is to be gained judicially by continuing the prosecution.

In another case, a young man in London, Ontario deliberately ran down a Pakistani family on June 6, 2021 killing four and seriously wounding one[90]. Initially charged with first degree murder and attempted murder, Nathaniel Veltman was later charged with terrorism. The case is still before Canadian courts.

There is a lively debate on whether the very small violent fringe of the incel "movement" (not necessarily an accurate term) constitutes terrorism or not. I personally see it as violent misogyny and it would be unwise to consider all misogynists as terrorists. Others disagree with me.

Another case in Canada has also been raised in this regard, that of the van attack in April 2018 by another alleged violent incel in Toronto, Alek Minassian, in which ten people were killed and another sixteen wounded. In March 2021 he was found guilty on ten counts of first-degree murder and 16 of attempted murders and later sentenced to life in prison on several concurrent sentences, with the possibility of parole after 25 years. If the February 2020 case is seen as terrorism, why was this earlier one not? As previously noted, there is no advantage from the perspective of the Crown to lay terrorism, rather than murder, charges. It is worth pointing out that in her verdict, the presiding judge noted that Minassian exaggerated about his links to incels in order to grant himself more notoriety.

It is noteworthy that my former employer, CSIS, wrote in its 2019 annual report that "violent misogyny" is a form of ideologically motivated extremism. It is far from clear that this move is necessary and furthermore raises questions over where the resources to monitor this violent phenomenon will come from. The CSIS I worked for was already overstretched: I cannot imagine what other priorities will suffer if the decision is made to investigate a handful of violent incels.

In addition, during my conversations with Naama Kates,[91] an American who looks at incels and has probably talked to more people who identify as such than anyone else on the planet, it became clear that a very, very small percentage of incels turn to violence. Ms. Kates indicated that it was all but inconceivable that the vast majority of non-violent individuals would ever take action of a violent nature. This is very different than the Islamist extremist crowd where there are hundreds of groups to join around the world and where violence is a central and necessary feature of their very being.

The debate on incels is an ongoing one but I am dismayed that, with the exception of Kates, very few who maintain that this is a form of terrorism have actually spoken with real-life "members" of this "movement." It may be that the handful who engage in acts of violence could be seen as terrorists by some, but this dichotomy does complicate how we see, analyse, and "deal with" incels as a whole.

But enough about incels. By the time this book is published much of this commentary may be obsolete. That there are right-wing extremists in Canada is not at issue. Several groups already exist here—the Proud Boys, the Three Percenters, La Meute (French for "the wolf pack"), and others. And in June 2019 Public Safety Canada for the first time listed a right-wing group as a terrorist entity, the neo-Nazi group Blood and Honour.[92] It is more than possible that members of these groups could carry out acts of violence which could be construed as terrorism.

In the wake of the January 2021 riot at the US Capitol, in which several members of the US Proud Boys took part, the Canadian government added this group to the listed terrorist entities a few weeks later (a coincidence?) despite the fact that this bunch had never done anything of a violent nature in Canada[93].

Then, in the wake of the 'Freedom Convoy' in Ottawa in January 2022—a dog's breakfast of anti-vaxxers, conspiracy theorists, angry misfits and others—there was more talk of the right-wing threat to Canada, again despite the lack of any violence during the "siege." That did not stop some Canadian politicians from calling this "terrorism" (which if most certainly was not!)[94]. Nevertheless, the Trudeau government invoked the Emergencies Act to bring an end to the 'occupation'. This had been the first time this tool had been used in Canadian history: its predecessor, the War Measures Act, had been invoked by Trudeau's father Pierre to give authorities extraordinary powers in October 1970 after the FLQ killed a provincial minister.

Recently there have been several incidents that have threatened to become violent. Actors from these fringes are obsessed and angry with a litany of issues: immigration (especially "irregular migration" from the US), COVID-19 (many believe the virus's effects have been exaggerated and the government's response overbearing), a general hate for Prime Minister Justin Trudeau, and the usual cast of characters: anti-Semitism, and Islamophobia. Any one of these could lead someone to lash out in an act of violence against perceived enemies.

Even the Canadian military acknowledges it has a problem with "racism and far-right activity" in its ranks. The former Chief of the Defence Staff, General Jon Vance, stated that the military is taking seriously the issue of extremists, and stressed that his forces have no room for vile ideologies, promising it would "boot out" anyone who was so inclined.[95]

And yet, the right-wing "problem" is nowhere near as serious in Canada as it is in the US, where the FBI and the Department of Homeland Security have publicly labelled it the number one threat. This determination is backed up by data: far more people in the US have been killed by right-wing extremists than by Islamist extremists in the post-9/11 period. One could even argue that the same applies here in Canada as more people have been killed by right-wing actions (six, all by Alexandre Bissonnette) than by jihadis (two, as described in the previous chapter), although it is important to count foiled attacks as well, all of which have been Islamist extremist in nature.

Interestingly, CSIS did investigate right-wing extremism in the 1990s. Most of the actors were tied to their US counterparts, and CSIS, according to my contact, had so successfully penetrated all the right-wing networks in Canada that they ceased to operate. Their American associates were particularly angry that the Canadians had allowed themselves to be foiled by Canada's "spies." To this day much of the Canadian far right "scene" is linked to that of the US, though this could change at some point in the future.

There was some activity by far-right actors in the 1980s as well, just as CSIS was seeing the light of day. The recession in North America in the early 1980s led to some anger among white supremacist and other right-wing extremists who wanted to overthrow the government, again predominantly in the US but with reach into Canada (mostly in the West as American right-wing extremists came north from Montana and Idaho). One contact told me that there were questions raised within the security intelligence community as to whether there was any real need to look at right-wing extremism at the time. As it turns out there was, but nothing led to any violent attacks during that period. I will weigh in on the infamous Grant Bristow and the Heritage Front investigation in the penultimate chapter.

Stewart Bell wrote about one Canadian right-wing extremist, Wolfgang Droege, from the days before CSIS was created, in his 2013 book, *Bayou of Pigs: The True Story of an Audacious Plot to Turn a Tropical Island into a Criminal Paradise*. Here is a summary of the book courtesy of Amazon. com:[96]

In 1981, a small but heavily armed force of misfits from Canada and the United States set off on a preposterous mission: invade an impoverished Caribbean country, overthrow its government in a coup d'état, install a puppet prime minister and transform the island into a crooks' paradise. Their leader was a Texas soldier of fortune named Mike Perdue. His lieutenant was a Canadian Nazi named Wolfgang Droege. Their destination: Dominica. For two years, they recruited fighting men, wooed investors, stockpiled weapons and forged links with the mob, leftist revolutionaries and militant Rastafarians. They called their invasion Operation Red Dog, and they were going to make millions. All that stood in their way were two federal agents from New Orleans on the biggest case of their lives.

Several Canadian academics have weighed in on the far-right problem in Canada and probably the best known is Dr. Barbara Perry of Ontario Tech University in Oshawa. In 2019 she published *Right-Wing Extremism in Canada* along with her then graduate student Ryan Scrivens (currently at Michigan State University). The two outlined the history of far-right extremism in Canada as well as hate crimes and ended with an appendix listing "Incidents related to Canadian right-wing extremists, 1980–2015." Dr Perry told me in an October 2020 podcast[97] that they had uncovered 150 such incidents, versus eight that are attributable to Islamist extremists in Canada over the same time period.

Upon reading this list, I was struck by how many were not even remotely related to terrorism. Most were hate crimes and would constitute harassment at best. While I am not downplaying the seriousness of hate crime, I also fail to see how the vast majority of these incidents compare in any way to the Toronto 18 plot to kill hundreds of people, the similarly vicious Canada Day plot in Victoria, or the attacks that resulted in the deaths of Warrant Officer Patrice Vincent and Corporal Nathan Cirillo two days apart in 2014. In other words, this data does not indicate that far-right terrorism constitutes a bigger problem in Canada than does the Islamist variety.

In my time at CSIS there were no significant right-wing extremism investigations of which I was aware in the security intelligence community. None. A fellow strategic analyst was asked to keep an eye on this threat part time along with his other duties. That was it. As noted above, I am certain that this has changed. As it should, given the rise (or in the case of Canada, re-emergence?) of right-wing extremist actors. It would be interesting to have some insight into how resources have been reallocated to cover this threat. Interestingly, in September 2020 a senior official from the Australian Security Intelligence Service, that nation's version of CSIS, stated that "far-right violent extremism" consumed up to 40 percent of that agency's counter-terrorism caseload, up from 10–15 percent before 2016.[98]

To those who believe that the security intelligence community has misallocated resources over the past two decades and should have devoted much more time and expense to the far right, I have a very simple response. If that is correct and we had been barking up the wrong tree, where in heaven's name are all the successful mass-casualty attacks?

We thwarted several Islamist terrorist plots that could have been catastrophic in nature. These investigations consumed a lot of time and effort. It stands to reason that, as a consequence, we did not have many investigations looking at right-wing extremism. It also stands to reason that if the "watchers" were not watching, these actors would have had free rein to cause mayhem and carnage. And yet they did not.

What does all this mean? Several things. Right-wing extremism simply did not pose a significant level of threat in the 2000s and 2010s. Whoever espoused these hateful views was either a) incompetent, b) not serious, c) cowardly, or d) all of the above. This was a very different scenario than what we saw among the jihadists. The latter were a) competent, b) serious, and c) willing to die.

With respect to right-wing extremism, subject matter specialists will weigh in to discuss this phenomenon—where it is and where it is headed—but they will also be constrained by the facts, or lack thereof. Simply stated, there are no facts to support the view that right-wing extremism constituted a major terrorist threat in the 2000s and 2010s.

An RCMP contact confided to me that they would undertake a quarterly assessment process, and that the inter-agency Criminal Intelligence Service Canada (CISC) was an important partner in this regard. The assessment process would take into consideration both individuals of concern, as well as the importance of the threat posed. Rankings were constantly updated. The contact also indicated that in the wake of 9/11, efforts against the far right (and far left for that matter) were seriously affected.

This debate will continue for years and both sides will have a case to make. The bottom line is that Canada has a very small number of jihadis who pose a threat, as well as a very small number of right-wing extremists who pose a threat, and security intelligence and law enforcement agencies will have to monitor and investigate both. Where to find the resources necessary to do so remains an open question.

Left-Wing Terrorism in Canada

When I was in high school in the 1970s one of my favourite rock bands was Heart, led by sisters Ann and Nancy Wilson. The group had megahits such as "Crazy on You," "Dreamboat Annie," and "Barracuda." I loved their music and was particularly proud that they were Canadian!

Except that they were not.

Members of the band were actually from Seattle, Washington, on the West Coast of the United States, and only became "Canadian" when they decided to move to Vancouver (probably illegally!) so that the male musicians could avoid conscription into the US Army to serve in Vietnam. In other words, they were draft dodgers. I don't care, I still like their songs.

Canada in the late 1960s and early 1970s was imbued with the same counterculture and "flower power" found south of the border. Maybe not to the same extent, but the pervasive influence of American culture on Canada meant that we read, saw, and consumed the same material that our American cousins did.

One thing that did not transfer as easily, however, was left-wing violent extremism. We in Canada did not suffer violence from such groups as the Black Panthers or the Weather Underground to the same degree as the US did. An RCMP Security Service contact told me that there were investigations into the Weather Underground in British Columbia in the 1970s, but those tended to focus on Americans living in, or visiting, Canada. Once arrested, these extremists were handed to US law enforcement officials at the Canada-US border.

So no, left-wing violent extremism has not found a comfortable home here. That is not to say it will not, a point I will return to at the end of this section. But have there been actual left-wing terrorist acts?

The answer is no, with one exception.

One of the more oddly named terrorist cells in Canadian history goes by the moniker "the Squamish Five," named for the town of Squamish located north of Vancouver on Canada's West Coast. What is it about the West Coast and left-wing extremism? Maybe that is why some Canadians call it the "left coast"!

So, who were the Squamish Five?

Firstly, and much to my surprise, there is a made-for-TV movie about them! According to IMDB,[99] The Squamish Five aired in 1988 and is described as a "docudrama about urban guerrillas." I could not find any more details on this production.

The group referred to itself as "Direct Action" but the name

Squamish Five has stuck. Consisting of two women and three men—Ann Hansen, Juliet Belmas, Brent Taylor, Doug Stewart, and Gerry Hannah—the quintet was allegedly frustrated by the accomplishments of "traditional" anti-war and women's rights activism in the late 1970s and early 1980s and decided to take a more "active" approach, which for them meant engaging in terrorism (although they would most likely not have referred to themselves as terrorists).

On May 31, 1982, the group blew up the Cheekye-Dunsmuir substation near Qualicum Beach on Vancouver Island, a hydroelectric project which had been criticised as environmentally unsound. This act caused $5 million in damages.

The group's next major bombing occurred six months later, on October 14, 1982. The target was a facility in Toronto owned by Litton Systems, which produced guidance components for American cruise missiles, capable of carrying nuclear weapons. The Squamish Five left a vehicle conspicuously at the Litton facility, with a countdown clock and a stick of dynamite placed on the hood, and phoned in a bomb threat. Litton staff did not treat the threat seriously and was slow to evacuate the facilities. When the bomb was detonated ten people were injured, some seriously, including a security guard who was crippled for life.

Several months later the Squamish Five joined up with a larger group known as the Wimmin's Fire Brigade, which was angry at society's treatment of women and, in particular, at laws condoning the sale of different types of pornography (including those involving violence). The Brigade bombed three Red Hot Video stores in Vancouver and in the aftermath the government changed the law on the sale of violent pornography (Red Hot Videos was also fined).

Not surprisingly, these acts led the RCMP to create a special task force to actively track the group and bring them to justice. Thanks to surveillance, the RCMP uncovered a plan by the group to drive up the Sea to Sky Highway (Highway 99, a major north-south highway in British Columbia) to one of their training areas. On the morning of January 20, 1983, the RCMP, disguised as a road construction crew, stopped the vehicle the five were travelling in and made arrests.

The members were tried and convicted and received sentences ranging from six years to life. All members of the Squamish Five are now free. Ann Hansen published her memoirs, entitled "Direct Action: Memoirs of an Urban Guerrilla," in 2001. She maintains that the group never intended to cause any personal injury, only property damage.[100]

An RCMP contact described this cell as an "anarchist-leftist" gang. The group was keen to carry out more attacks on the Canadian military and planned several robberies of banks and Brinks trucks to fund future action, none of which came to fruition. Surveillance on the members of the group uncovered plans to kill security guards if necessary. What some may dismiss as a small collection of wannabes was, on the contrary, a group of violent Canadians bent on death and destruction.

The Squamish Five is a good example of what happened when counter-subversion was dropped as an investigative priority (section 2(d) of the CSIS Act). The decision was made to morph it into counterterrorism (section 2(c) of the CSIS Act). It was never an investigative priority, but the security intelligence community did its due diligence in this regard.

Coastal Link Gas Attack

On February 17, 2022 at least twenty people armed with axes and torches attacked a campsite belonging to Calgary-based Coastal GasLink, causing millions of dollars in damages[101]. Mask-clad attackers tried to burn a truck with an employee inside. The incident occurred in the middle of the night and was condemned by First Nations leaders and Prime Minister Trudeau[102].

As there have been 'incidents' between anti-pipeline activists and the company's employees it is reasonable to assume that the attack was planned: whether the perpetrators were environmentalists or First Nations has yet to be determined. At this juncture, it is clear that the violence was intended to send a political message: hence it could fall within Canada's terrorism laws.

Church Burnings

Canada's history with its First Nations (which our American friends call 'native Americans') is a sorry one. Decades of mistreatment, stolen land, marginalization and other decisions have left this percentage of the Canadian population (approximately 5%) underserviced and beset with high rates of drug abuse, alcoholism and criminality. Of course these ills are not solely attributable to historical actions but they were certainly aided and abetted by them.

One of the most egregious actors in this regard was the Roman Catholic Church. In conjunction with government policy, the church removed children from their homes and placed them in 'residential schools', where they were physically, emotionally and sexually abused. The discovery of mass graves in recent years at the sites of former schools has only aggravated the sadness and anger.

Possibly in response, several Catholic churches have been burned, some completely, in Canada[103]. The culprits are, as of the time of writing, unknown and RCMP investigations are continuing.

Could these have constituted acts of terrorism? Wow!

If these acts of arson are tied to First Nations angry at the mistreatment of their communities for decades could this not be construed as a 'political' act? If so, there is a strong argument that terrorism charges could be laid under the Canadian Criminal Code. Not that the Trudeau government would touch that with a ten-foot (three-metre) pole!

Summary

As already noted, terrorism takes multiple forms. The ideas and ideology underpinning terrorists and terrorist groups cover the entire political spectrum from left to right, and also include religious and ethno-national justifications. The types of right- and left-wing terrorism discussed here are merely a small sample of what has happened and what will most likely continue to happen around the world, albeit not necessarily in Canada.

In the years to come it is possible that today's far right-wing groups—La Meute, the Three Percenters and others—as well as new ones, will expand their activities and become more dangerous. It is equally possible that we may never see another mass casualty attack in Canada on the scale of the murders in the Québec City mosque.

With respect to the far left we have yet to see any definitive significant violent action by those narrowly defined by such motivations. Should the Canadian government, or Canadian companies, especially those in the resource extraction industries, continue to drag their feet on measures to slow global warming and climate change, it is indeed possible that a fringe element will resort to violence.

In any event it is far from certain that either movement will engage in mass-casualty attacks. It will be interesting to see, to the extent possible given secrecy and "operational need-to-know," how CSIS, the RCMP, and others deal with these challenges in the years to come.

5

Counterterrorism Challenges

THIS SHORT CHAPTER WILL EXAMINE certain aspects of counterterrorism in Canada that usually remain in the shadows, but which occasionally see the light of day and lead to debate and criticism of how we do national security. Each of them is complicated, and the goal here is to demonstrate just how difficult they are, and yet are integral parts of counterterrorism investigations.

Relationships with Foreign Partners

I will never forget my very first day at CSE—June 13, 1983. I had successfully applied for a position as a multilingual analyst with what I thought was the Department of National Defence (DND). In those days, CSE did not advertise and obscured its mission within DND. In fact, I had no real idea what I was getting myself into as my employer could not share specifics with me in the absence of the required security clearance.

Shortly after obtaining that clearance, accepting the position, and finishing my MA at the UWO, I moved to Ottawa to begin my new career. As my start day dawned, I put on my one suit, a dark blue three-piece outfit (this was 1983 after all!) and bused to the Sir Leonard Tilley Building in the south part of town. I was ushered into a room where I met one of the largest and most imposing men I had ever met, who was a former RCMP officer and the head of internal security for CSE.

He walked me through what CSE actually did, that is, signals intelligence, and as he spoke, I must confess to feeling a combination of wonder and fear. This "DND" I had applied to was actually a spy organisation and before then I had no idea that Canada even had one. He concluded the indoctrination with the admonition that if I were to wrongfully disclose the content of my work with anyone not having a "need to know" I would get "fourteen years in the slammer."

I went home a little shaken after that. Among the many new concepts and realities bestowed on me that day was the existence of the "Five Eyes." What sounded like a beast from the imagination of J. R. R. Tolkien was actually a very exclusive club of nations which agreed to share intelligence among themselves. Created in the aftermath of World War II, its members were: Australia, Canada, New Zealand, the UK and the US. In other words, the world's largest Western anglophone nations.

Sharing within the Five Eyes is unprecedented. Very sensitive intelligence, including the most secretive SIGINT, is routinely distributed among the partners. Not everything is available to all, of course. Each nation reserves the right to limit its finished (and raw) intelligence to its own clients (known in the US as NOFORN, or in Canada as Canadian Eyes Only), or to a subset of the five. In the 1980s New Zealand found itself cut off from much US intelligence pursuant to its policy of asking whether visiting US naval vessels were carrying nuclear weapons, as the US policy was "don't ask don't tell." Still, it is a very strong alliance.

Within the Five Eyes, the US was clearly the majority shareholder by virtue of its huge intelligence community, which includes the National Security Agency (NSA), the CIA, and satellite imagery, among others. The UK held second place, Canada third, and Australia fourth. New Zealand brought up the rear. All members had their niche programs supported largely by their unique geographic advantages. For instance, Australia had great insight into Southeast Asia while Canada had a beneficial vantage point into the Union of Soviet Socialist Republics (USSR) thanks to our northern position. The intercept station known as Alert on Ellesmere Island is a mere 817 kilometres from the North Pole, just across the top of the world from the USSR. Thus, while Canadian intelligence consumers received much more from our allies than we gave, we nevertheless made a valued contribution.

As long as the Five Eyes has been around there have arisen calls for the "club" to admit new members. I was aware of the occasional meeting of a larger gathering of SIGINT nations: after all, we all knew that this capability was not restricted to the five Anglo countries. According to a Guardian article in July 2020, some UK Members of Parliament have argued that the alliance "could be expanded to include Japan and broadened into a strategic economic relationship that pools key strategic reserves such as critical minerals and medical supplies."[104]

When I moved from CSE to CSIS I was introduced to a much larger intelligence sharing network. In one of my earliest meetings with a foreign agency I recall turning to a colleague and asking "Can we share with them? They're not part of the Five Eyes." I was reassured that all was well since CSIS had entered into a "Section 17" arrangement with the agency in question.

Section 17 of the CSIS Act authorises the Service to share and receive intelligence with any intelligence or security agency which has received sign-off from two ministers. It reads:

(1) For the purpose of performing its duties and functions under this Act, the Service may,

(a) with the approval of the Minister, enter into an arrangement or otherwise cooperate with

(i) any department of the Government of Canada or the government of a province or any department thereof, or

(ii) any police force in a province, with the approval of the Minister responsible for policing in the province; or

(b) with the approval of the Minister after consultation by the Minister with the Minister of Foreign Affairs, enter into an arrangement or otherwise cooperate with the government of a foreign state or an institution thereof or an international organisation of states or an institution thereof.

During my time with CSIS we had agreements with hundreds of such agencies. I was fortunate to meet with many of them, both in Ottawa and in their host countries.

Some of these foreign services could be described as akin to the Five Eyes partners: Western, democratic, and abiding by all international human rights protocols. Others were not. This raised a conundrum: could (or should) CSIS share intelligence with an agency which could then use it to abuse someone's human rights, such as through the use of torture or unfair detention?

There is no need for me to go into the details of this challenge. The 2008 Iacobucci Commission, an inquiry which found that Canada had shared intelligence with the Syrian government which proceeded to torture three Canadians, all of whom later received large financial settlements, is part of the public record and I will not delve further into that case. It is still true, however, that this issue is much more complicated than presented in that record.

A former CSIS official suggested that on occasion you are forced to deal with another agency whose record is anything but spotless (the actual quote was "sometimes you have to dance with the ugly partner"). You do so with the full knowledge that there are serious concerns, and you try to ensure that the receiver will respect human rights, and so a caveat stating such accompanies all shared material.

Some would argue that this attitude is supportive of torture in the pursuit of intelligence. Nothing could be farther from the truth. There are those who maintain that the ends justify the means, but in this instance, it refers to getting intelligence which could serve in preventing a mass casualty terrorist attack.

I will leave the discussion concerning the morality of these matters to philosophers and human rights specialists. The simple truth, however, is that Canada gets much more intelligence than it provides and hence must enter into intelligence-sharing agreements with other countries, not just the Five Eyes, with whom we share similar world views and values.

Besides, even if the Five Eyes appears to be a club of the like-minded, how can we forget what happened to Maher Arar, a Canadian engineer rendered by the US government to Syria in the wake of 9/11 based on information that he was a terrorist? If we cannot trust the Americans to not use our intelligence for purposes of this sort, whom can we trust?

The most important point to make is that counterterrorism is an international problem. All countries are threatened by it and all countries have a shared interest in protecting their citizens from death and injury and their infrastructure from destruction.

This common challenge necessitates information sharing and, where necessary and feasible, joint operations. While this is easier among like-minded powers, it is much more fraught with danger when powers that are not like-minded are brought to the table. Security agencies in democracies must carefully consider the risks involved and weigh the benefits of greater knowledge vs. possible human rights abuses.

As mentioned, CSIS would share intelligence with the proviso that human rights will be protected. Some would retort that it is ludicrous to expect a state such as Syria to abide by such restrictions. Maybe. On the other hand, were a terrorist act to occur when intelligence was absent and could have been obtained from a country that does not share our Westminster form of democratic government, what would the public's reaction be then?

Of potential relevance here is the "ticking bomb" scenario, which has been considered in ethical debates about whether torture is ever justified. It goes something like this (thanks to the BBC for this version):[105]

- A terrorist group states that it has concealed a nuclear bomb in London.
- The authorities have captured the leader of the group.
- He says that he knows where the bomb is.
- He refuses to reveal the location.
- Torture is guaranteed to produce the information needed to ensure the authorities find and make the bomb safe.

This dilemma is rare: I never came across it in my career. Nevertheless, intelligence sharing among nations has happened, is happening, and will continue to happen for the simple reason that it is helpful. No one nation can do this on its own, not even the US. We owe it to our citizens to gather the best information, be it intelligence and/or evidence, to keep them safe.

A contact told me that in the post-9/11 period, the need to share widely became the norm. In comparison to earlier years in which there was perhaps a reluctance to give intelligence to some allies, the new paradigm was to share more, with the appropriate caveats in place for its use. As the contact said, "you had to have a very good reason not to provide this information to _____." (Fill in the name of a partner agency.) The global nature of the terrorist threat and the recognition that we had to give to receive, clearly drove this evolution in thinking.

There is another matter that should be raised. Once you share a piece of intelligence with a given partner agency you effectively lose control of it. All the caveats are worth little once you hand something to another nation's service, and that service decides that it is in its national security interest to share it further.

At the end of the day the underlying question we posed to ourselves was, "If we do not share and someone dies, what then?" The reports written by analysts, including me, were accompanied by a matrix for the analyst to record the foreign intelligence services that could receive that piece of assessed intelligence. Each choice of foreign agency had to be carefully considered based on the content and the implications for bilateral relations. And yet, I heard time and time again that shared intelligence was "currency." As noted above, we had to pay our dues to get future benefits in the form of intelligence from those partners. In the words of a contact, "we are a net importer of intelligence." For the record, other Government of Canada agencies also saw the need to share with allies. The effort put into creating and maintaining relationships with foreign partners is worthwhile and pays dividends down the road.

One anecdote. It was relayed to me that a leading Canadian human rights advocate stated that if a piece of information could possibly have been derived from torture it should not be used, even if it could help save the lives of one or many Canadians. While I respect that individual's point of view, it is not as cut and dried as some might think. As a contact told me, "this is a wicked problem" (that is, one that is difficult or impossible to solve due to several possible factors, including incomplete or contradictory information, the number of opinions involved, and the interconnectedness of the problem with other problems). Another contact put it to me more bluntly: "I would have had a relationship with the Devil himself if it would save the life of a Canadian."

The Use of Human Sources or Agents

The recruitment and deployment of human sources (the CSIS term) or agents (the RCMP term) is the bread and butter of security intelligence and law enforcement agencies. Yes, electronic intercept—either locally through court-authorised warrants or internationally through SIGINT—is important, as is physical surveillance and, on occasion, satellite imagery (called IMINT), but there is nothing like a human source. You can have a person infiltrate a group or a cell and can further have that person follow up on certain points and pursue lines of inquiry. Intercept is hit or miss—like casting a net, you get what you get.

I would like to think that it is obvious to everyone that the people recruited to act in this function are not drawn from Mother Theresa and the Sisters of Charity. Sources have to be believable to the terrorists who are about to be spied upon. This means that these individuals themselves may have "iffy" backgrounds (criminal, ideological, etc.). It is of course important to ensure to the extent possible that these sources are trustworthy and can be relied upon to carry out the instructions given. There is, after all, a history of sources who were double, or even triple agents.

Some see this as problematic. I see it as the cost of doing business. Highly placed human sources need to fit in and sell themselves to the "targets." Those who fail to do so or whose cover is blown could end up dead. I admire those who take these risks to help keep us safe. Sure, some do it for money, but most see the importance of what this entails.

It would be remiss of me not to say something about Grant Bristow and the Heritage Front debacle of the 1990s. The Heritage Front was Canada's leading white supremacist organisation at the time and Bristow was the CSIS source who infiltrated the group. The case went public and much criticism was placed on CSIS for having worked with such an unsavoury character. The reader is encouraged to look into the affair, much of which has been widely reported.[106]

Bristow made an excellent source precisely because of his unsavouriness. He was able to infiltrate several groups precisely because he could sell himself as a true right-wing extremist. That is what an intelligence service or law enforcement agency looks for. The source or agent has to "talk the talk" to be credible and provide useful information to handlers. Bristow's access was remarkable and shook the far-right movements to their core. They realised that they were that deeply penetrated. What else do you want a security service to do?

Intelligence versus Evidence

Some countries have opted to fold security intelligence into law enforcement agencies. The FBI in the US, SAEPO in Sweden and PST in Norway are good examples.

Canada has chosen to play the game differently. In the decision to create CSIS in 1984 by removing security intelligence from the RCMP and placing it in a new civilian agency, we ended up with a hybrid system, one that works well enough—most of the time. An RCMP contact noted that this arrangement was right for Canada and that no one has seriously looked at recombining law enforcement and intelligence agencies.

CSIS collects intelligence and shares its findings with its government partners. This information is not gathered in an "evidentiary" fashion, i.e., it cannot and must not form part of a criminal case that could go to court. CSIS information can help inform, and sometimes lead, a partner agency, but that information must remain secret and not used in a criminal investigation.

The way I like to portray this is that CSIS, by virtue of its mandate to investigate based on "reasonable grounds to suspect"—a lower threshold than the RCMP's "reasonable grounds to believe"—acts as a "Psst! Hey you! Look over here!" In other words, what CSIS learns can help others, usually the RCMP, in its own independent efforts to investigate criminal activity. CSIS and the RCMP do not carry out joint investigations, but they can do "parallel" ones. This of course requires good communication between the two agencies to ensure efficiency and non-interference.

To date, the need for CSIS information to remain out of the public eye has worked out well. That may be changing. An ongoing terrorism trial in Ottawa may upset this arrangement. The defence in the Awso Peshdary case asked for access to CSIS human source files and the judge was considering such at the time of writing. An RCMP contact told me that he would be "shocked" if the judge would order such a disclosure.

Forcing CSIS to submit its intelligence to the courts would be an unmitigated disaster in my view. Many individuals are happy to work for CSIS as human sources or in other ways precisely because there is no risk they will have to appear in court and testify. Some fear that possibility as they believe it will put them in personal danger. Others simply don't want the publicity or the public judgment of their actions. This may matter in certain communities where talking to the "spies" can lead to condemnation and rejection.

If Canada can no longer guarantee that CSIS intelligence will remain sealed the agency may be hard pressed to continue its successful work. On the other hand, defendants have a right to see all the information that contributed to the charges against them. Perhaps there are ways to do this differently: after all, the security services in other countries seem to have resolved this conundrum.

One contact told me that the issue of "intelligence to evidence" has been discussed for decades. It never seems to get to the point in Canada where a decision is made, and we can emulate the arrangements made by some of our major Western allies which have resolved this issue. Like cold fusion, a solution to this challenge always seems to be five years away.

Where intelligence cannot be disclosed, the information has to be recreated, i.e., collected in a way that meets evidentiary standards. This takes time. In a perfect world the intelligence could be shared and used to contribute toward a successful prosecution. Alas, the advice that has dominated to date in Canada has been to keep the two separate!

Another instance where the intelligence/evidence firewall has proven ill-suited to decision-making in Canada is that of the "national security certificates." These documents are actually issued by the immigration department in Canada and assert that, based on information received, including intelligence, a given individual is deemed to pose a threat to national security and should be removed. It is important to stress that these people are not Canadian citizens and have no inherent right to remain in Canada.

To date, very few of these cases have succeeded insofar as those deemed a security threat have been deported: in fact, one individual, Mohamed Harkat, was still fighting extradition to his native Algeria as of July 2020, although he was placed on a certificate in 2002.[107] Lawyers, and a bevy of supporters, maintain that sending these men (they have all been men) back to their homelands—usually North Africa, the Middle East, or Asia— would be the same as a death sentence or at a minimum exposure to torture. Indeed, the track records of many of these nations is far from stellar. Added to this is the conviction that the security services are either "making things up" or are racists (or Islamophobic). Hence, according to this reasoning, all these men were poor innocents caught up in a security net.

However, to my mind, these supporters are the equivalent of what used to be called, in the Cold War days, "useful idiots" (i.e., those who defended Marxist-Leninism and communism despite the threat those systems posed to Western democracies). That assessment may strike some as harsh, but I believe it is accurate, nonetheless.

In my experience (of note, I was involved in four cases), the intelligence used to call for removal was based on security intelligence investigations and data shared by allies. This information was given to the court in two files: one that contained the sensitive intelligence, and one provided to the defendant in which the sensitive intelligence was removed or "sanitised."

This intelligence was solid, corroborated, and tied crucially to the activities of the individuals who represented national security threats. Most of them belonged to known terrorist groups abroad. And yet, despite the completeness of the dossiers, none of these individuals were removed. In fact one, Adil Charkaoui, was granted Canadian citizenship; nonetheless he continues to surface in open media in conjunction with Islamist extremism (see the case of the Montreal teen ISIS wannabes above). They are all still here and some cases are still evolving, twenty years later!

In an effort to make the process "fairer," the Canadian government tried to create the position of amicus curiae ("friend of the court"). Lawyers were given security clearances and allowed to see the sensitive intelligence in order to act on the defendant's behalf. Regardless, intelligence could not be challenged adequately, especially where it was received from an allied service.

The whole system is a mess and there is no solution in sight. To my mind, Canada and Canadians should have the ability to choose who becomes one of us, and yet even those known to have terrorist affiliations cannot be denied residency. What does it say about a government when it is unable to make decisions on national security?

The national security certificates were a bad idea from day one. What should have been a decision made during the immigration process became one that brought in security intelligence information in a very public way. The people held on security certificates should have been removed from Canada as soon as it was learned who they really were. Had this information been accessible before they landed in Canada, they would have been denied permission to be here in the first place, as undoubtedly happens thousands of times a year at Canadian embassies and consular offices abroad. The five Muslim men alleged to have terrorist ties should have been treated in analogous fashion.

Data Volumes and Encryption

In the late 1990s I headed a team of a dozen or so analysts responsible for collection and data flow at CSE. The section was responsible for all the raw data through which the linguists had to troll to find the nuggets of information that would be turned into an intelligence product and provided to government clients.

The data flow manager used to describe this process as "drinking from a firehose," as there was far too much data for anyone to go through to seek the relevant pieces. Yes, we had algorithms to help with this task, and I imagine that the CSE of 2023 bears little resemblance to that of 1998, but I also know that the volumes of data available worldwide has also increased by orders of magnitude. It is a battle that the intelligence world cannot win.

When there is too much to look at, inevitably mistakes will be made. Important pieces of information go unseen (or unheard), unanalysed, and unshared. It is likely that some terrorist attacks succeed, at least in part, because the agencies tasked with stopping them cannot stay on top of everything.

Sadly, the situation is likely to get worse, much worse. New online platforms seem to pop up every day and the numbers of people that subscribe to them and post material, most of which is absolutely useless and of no interest or consequence to anyone, is also growing exponentially. The interconnectivity is on the one hand a marvelous development in human history as more people have access to information that can have positive effects on their lives. On the other, it makes intelligence work, and more narrowly counterterrorism work, that much harder.

I am sure that there are technical solutions for some of this and artificial intelligence gains can only help. And yet there is something to be said for the human ability to detect deception and intent, both of which are what security intelligence and law enforcement agencies are good at.

One further point concerns the encryption problem. For a brief period in the late 1980s I worked as a multilingual cryptanalyst at CSE. In those days we were still able to break certain cypher systems (which ones I cannot divulge for obvious reasons). As the 1990s progressed it became ever more difficult to do so as encryption became harder and the codebreakers could not match their targets. While I cannot say for certain as I have not had access to this part of the game for three decades, I would bet that today, once the material is encrypted, decryption is virtually impossible.

Suffice to say that the amount of information available to counterterrorism specialists is swamping these officials. And it will get worse.

Resource Allocation

In the immediate aftermath of 9/11 those agencies in the security intelligence and law enforcement counterterrorism business "made out like bandits." By that I mean they got a lot more money and human resources to put toward investigations. CSIS grew; for example, the number of yearly intake classes for intelligence officers increased. This was very different than the situation a decade earlier, at the time of the fall of the Soviet Union and its allies, where the much ballyhooed "peace dividend" would mean we would no longer need intelligence and could pare back on staff. There were cutbacks to intelligence agencies in the wake of our "victory" over the communists.

Governments around the world were so shocked by the events in New York and Washington that they wanted to do everything possible to prevent a repeat performance. It is also probable they realised that if a second wave transpired, the national support and sense of purpose natural in the aftermath of a tragedy of such proportion would dissipate.

CSE provides a good example. When I moved from CSE to CSIS, the former was somewhere in the neighbourhood of 1,000 employees. Within a relatively short period of time that number had doubled (and is now above 3,000 I believe). In addition, CSE also assumed a counterterrorism role, one it never had before 9/11.

The RCMP also grew and created the INSETs (see Chapter 1).

Fast forward to 2023. At the time of writing COVID-19 is still ravaging much of the world. Governments are going trillions of dollars into debt to keep their economies going. While that money must be repaid at some future point it is arguably the right thing to do at this juncture.

These funds are most assuredly not going to counterterrorism efforts, even though terrorist groups are still very active around the world and show no signs of letting up. This is not going to change any time soon. Consequently, terrorists have greater freedom to plan and kill.

Further complicating matters during this time of pandemic is the probable restriction on the number of officers who can be in the office at any one time to prevent the further spread of the virus. The nature of counterterrorism work, including the secret classification of much of the information used to conduct investigations, means that "working from home," an option for many in both the private and public sectors who toil on open information, does not apply here.

Fewer resources able to keep tabs on terrorists could result in more attacks. It is still far too early to make this determination as of the fall of 2020 but anecdotally, at least, there appear to be successful attacks occurring in many countries around the world.

Additionally, at any given moment security intelligence and law enforcement agencies are pulled in multiple directions: court appearances, ATIP ("access to information policy") requests, putting out fires. All these take time and attention away from investigations. This is not to say that these other issues are not important, but they cannot compare with life and death situations.

And one more detail. The "rise" of far-right terrorism—not an accurate or useful term but let's go with it—is putting pressure on security intelligence and law enforcement agencies to do more with less. The constant struggle to allocate resources to counterterrorism priorities is not easy. The adage "robbing Peter to pay Paul" applies here to a large extent. Decisions to focus on one part of the threat spectrum at the expense of another are made in the hope that a) they are the correct ones, and b) that the other part of the spectrum will not surge at the same time. Both CSIS and the RCMP have these challenges: as an RCMP contact told me "we never had enough resources to do everything."

As already noted, those that work in security intelligence and law enforcement in a counterterrorism capacity are held to a high standard. Mistakes are not acceptable since these may entail loss of life. We never have enough resources to do it all and yet we are expected to do so. As one CSIS contact explained to me, at the time of the Ressam affair the security intelligence community was working flat out on with Sikh extremism, Tamil extremism, Islamist extremism, and other files. These agencies simply never have enough bodies to cover all eventualities.

Public Perception and Community Support

It has been my experience in Canada that the average citizen neither understands nor cares about terrorism. Don't get me wrong: this is a good thing to a certain extent. Obsessing about what is a relatively minor scourge would not be helpful.

At the same time, however, this lack of understanding and appreciation for what counterterrorism forces do is worrisome. As noted in the introduction, when we "get it right," i.e., nothing happens because terrorist cells are infiltrated and neutralised, no one tends to notice; but when the opposite happens, all hell breaks loose, and fingers are pointed in our direction. Since most of the work that goes into counterterrorism is sensitive and rarely, if ever, made public (even in trials), the citizenry never really accepts the role we play.

The focus on our "mistakes," real or perceived, has the knock-on effect of employee demoralisation in the relevant agencies. If you only make the headlines when it is assumed you messed up, is it any wonder that morale can suffer? I do maintain that those on the inside will continue their efforts regardless of the views of their fellow Canadians; but some recognition on occasion would be nice.

One particular aspect of community buy-in has had a disproportionate effect. In the aftermath of 9/11, much of the counterterrorism focus settled on Islamist extremism, and for good reason. Not only were the hijackers that day all Islamist terrorists but we were seeing many others, some "homegrown" and others linked to groups abroad.

This effort led to accusations of "Islamophobia." There were those in some Muslim communities in Canada who felt, and stated openly, that we were targeting Canadian Muslims merely because of their faith (rather than based on "reasonable grounds to suspect" a threat to national security). This was clearly a false assumption, but it stuck.

Not having a good relationship with a community engenders several follow-on disadvantages:

- Communities are less willing to report suspicious activity.
- Community members are less willing to express an interest in the security intelligence and law enforcement field.
- Fewer people are willing to work as sources/informants, and those that do suffer in their communities (Mubin Shaikh is a good example, see Chapter 3).

CSIS and the RCMP did a tremendous job at bridge-building after 9/11. I contributed to such efforts and can attest to the sincerity with which they were undertaken. Were they perfect? Of course not. Could there have been individuals who really were Islamophobic? Probably. The vast majority, however, were honest Canadians trying to do their part in keeping Canada safe.

I could simply state that every Canadian has a duty to help CSIS and the RCMP keep us safe. But I'd rather say that we need to work together, and that both sides have to make concessions, for by cooperating and collaborating we can go much further to prevent bad things from taking place.

My experience in what is called "Countering Violent Extremism" (CVE) while at Public Safety Canada was mixed. Some communities welcomed us and were keen to have an in-depth dialogue on terrorism and national security. Others accused us of only showing up when something went "bang."

Does CVE actually work? No one knows. Millions of dollars have been spent, not only in Canada, and there is little to no data that establishes what are effective practices and what are not. The interest in CVE took off after 9/11: it is far from certain that the funds allocated have been wisely spent.

Political Correctness in CounterTerrorism?

As we have seen throughout this book, 'terrorism' is a loaded term. To be labeled as such invites possible legal action, public opprobrium, and possible hate-driven reactions. It is thus crucial that the term be used wisely so as not to feed prejudices and further unhelpful reactions.

Still, the word does carry weight and it is also crucial to be as accurate as possible in using the proper terms for the various types of terrorism that exist. Different groups and individuals have different motives and in order to understand these motivations it is necessary to apply the right term to the right movement.

Recall that in the Canadian Criminal Code (section 83.01) terrorism is defined as an act of violence perpetrated for 'political, ideological, or religious' purpose. Note that nowhere are the terms 'political, ideological, or religious' defined: this is problematic.

The Trudeau government decided somewhere in 2017 to alter the terminology it uses to refer to terrorism. Instead of using phrases such as 'Islamist terrorism', 'Sikh terrorism' or 'right-wing terrorism', it has imposed the overly generic phrases IMVE (ideologically motivated violent extremism), PMVE (politically motivated violent extremism) and RMVE (religiously motivated violent extremism). As some have said, this reflects the language of the criminal code.

And it is wrong, unnecessary, inaccurate and probably a child of political correctness. Allow me to explain:[108].

- Firstly, the terminology is so broad as to be meaningless. Who decides what is 'ideological'? What is a 'political objective'? Is there any agreement on any of this?
- The fact that there are some terrorist groups — such as ISIS and Al Qaeda — which are simultaneously ideological, political AND religious undermines the accuracy of the adopted terminology;
- By using generic wording we fail to get at the specifics of what is occurring. What are the differences between ISIS, say, and the

Proud Boys? What are the similarities? This is what analysis is all about;

- The use of RMVE suggests that ANY religion can lead someone to engage in violence. While this is true in theory it is a fact that the one faith most behind terrorism in 2022 is Islam;

- More narrowly, one of the criticisms over the use of the term 'Islamist terrorism' was that it tied Islam to violence, a claim many Muslims described as inaccurate. The choice of RMVE, ostensibly to remove this link, is actually feeding it!

- The older use of 'Islamist terrorism' has a long history in security and academic fields worldwide. Note that 'Islamist' is not the same as 'Islamic'

- We in the security industry have made our own alterations over the decades in the words we used to describe terrorist groups. In the early 2000s we labeled Al Qaeda and others 'Sunni Islamic Terrorism' (to differentiate them from Shia Muslim groups like Hizballah). We shifted to 'Islamist terrorism' in the late 2000s to reflect other usages.

I am fairly confident that the new nomenclature should not have any effect on those investigating terrorism (although my departure from CT operations in 2013 precludes any certainty on my part). Nevertheless, these changes strike me as political correctness and it is not inconceivable that there could be some political interference on our security intelligence and law enforcement agencies. That would not be a good development.

Do we even need terrorism laws?

It may strike some as odd in a book on terrorism in Canada over the last century and a half that the author is even asking this question. Of course we need laws to deal with terrorism since terrorism is a real issue, both in Canada and internationally.

But do we?

Recall that terrorism was not in the Canadian Criminal Code prior to December 2001 despite there having been attacks in the country for 133 years prior to the addition. Courts were able to prosecute terrorists successfully using other parts of the Code—was the new section that important.

In addition there are two parts to a criminal offence in classic legal jargon: mens rea and actus reus. The former refers to the motivation behind a crime; the latter to the actual crime itself. The latter is easier to prove beyond reasonable doubt: either an act occurred or it did not. The former requires a degree of mind reading—why did the suspect carry out the crime? In some cases suspects provide their thinking behind the decision to kill (if they can be believed), either through a confession or some kind of manifesto they post online. In other cases it is next to impossible to determine motive.

Since, under Canadian sentencing practices, there is no distinction between 1st degree murder and terrorism—they both carry a maximum life sentence, what is gained by adding the burden of motive to the trial? We dealt with terrorism for a very long time without a requisite offence in that name and could just as easily do so in the future.

Note that none of this affects the ability of CSIS or the RCMP to investigate terrorists and terrorist plots. Not having recourse to a terrorism offence does not prevent gathering intelligence/evidence and eventually moving to prosecution. The only change is in the actual charge to be laid.

Some would argue that terrorism is "special," that it is a particularly horrendous crime that needs a separate part of the Code. Tell that to the parents of Sandy Hook Elementary School in Connecticut where a mass shooting, that was NOT terrorist in nature, took the lives of 26 people (twenty of whom were children). The crime was heinous enough without the need to bring in a terrorism label.

A Developing Intelligence Culture

I'll end this brief chapter with a lament. My country, Canada, which I love dearly, has a severely underdeveloped intelligence culture. In my experience, many government officials have neither an appreciation for nor an understanding of intelligence, whether that applies to counterterrorism or other threats.

In this, Canada is quite different from its closest allies, the UK and the US. Both of these countries spend much more money per capita on intelligence than Canada does, and they make much better use of it. We have much to learn from them, in part because they both have longer histories in this endeavour (especially the UK).

This is not to say that no one welcomed the contribution intelligence could make. I distinctly recall officials who would delay decisions until they had had a chance to see the latest intelligence. These individuals, alas, were few and far between.

When it came to terrorism the same applied. CSIS was giving briefings on Islamist extremism "downtown" beginning in the early 2000s, and my impression was that many of our clients shrugged at our analysis. I cannot discern why this was the case: it simply was.

At the risk of being repetitive, of course we did not have all the answers, but we did have some of them. Sidelining what we had to offer, regardless of the reason, was not an intelligent, or wise thing to do.

Are matters better now? From what I hear from those still in the business, it seems not. Simply put, the Canadian government has to get better at using intelligence. That little has changed since my time there speaks volumes.

The following example, though not tied to terrorism, is particularly illustrative. As we continue to live through COVID-19, accusations have arisen that the government instructed staff at the Global Public Health Intelligence Network (GPHIN)—tasked for decades with the early detection of health outbreaks and providing continuing surveillance as they worsened to assist with government decision-making—to ignore SIGINT and rely exclusively on what foreign counterparts were saying officially.[109]

This brings back memories, many of them sad. Canadian officials who were cleared to read intelligence regularly dismissed Canada's own contributions, instead favouring what our Five Eyes partners had to say. If the allegations concerning GPHIN are correct, if officials truly told their analysts to "focus on official information, instead of working with 'informal' information," then that failing is still very much alive.

That being said, one contact told me that he had seen a sea change with government clients after 2000. Whether that was tied to the events of 9/11 or not, there was a greater appetite for CSIS intelligence product, which spoke to a recognition that CSIS and other intelligence, both raw and assessed, was beginning to be appreciated more. Nevertheless, there were still senior officials who did not understand intelligence and were even ignorant as to how large the intelligence organisations were. One contact told me that in the immediate post-9/11 period, one such official pushed back against a request for more resources by asking CSIS why it could not do the job assigned to it with "10,000 employees": the actual number was fewer than 2,000.

Canadian intelligence agencies are world class and admired by their allied partners. That our own government may not be among those admirers is unfortunate and constitutes a dereliction of its duties to use all available data to make better decisions to keep Canada and Canadians safe and to protect our interests.

Summary

Security intelligence is a complicated business. There are a lot of moving parts, constantly changing priorities and government requirements, a need to work in secret, and a public that has a poor understanding of how it all comes together (hint: it is not all James Bond!). The bits that relate to counterterrorism are perhaps even more complicated.

Unlike counter-intelligence, counterterrorism is carried out to prevent things from going boom in the night, and people from dying. The need to detect, monitor, and interdict terrorists before they act is not just a task: it is the only one.

What security intelligence and law enforcement agencies need in order to accomplish this is often not well understood. This short chapter is an attempt to look at the issues and challenges facing those who prevent terrorism. It is hoped that the issues and challenges presented here give the reader a slightly more nuanced appreciation for the difficulty of this work.

6
Final Thoughts

AS I PEN THESE LAST WORDS it strikes me that the manuscript for this book is a little more than 200 pages. Canada is, as of the time of writing, 155 years old. Which means that I have distilled a century and a half of terrorism history in my country to one year and a bit per page.

Of course, it is a little more complicated than that. Recall that the first terrorist attack occurred in 1868 and the next one did not happen until the 1960s. In other words, almost a full century passed between attack number one and attack number two. When put that way, it is an outstanding statistic.

If this were a book on terrorism in Afghanistan (or Iraq or Nigeria or Syria or . . .) I would have had to devote each page to a given day or week. A book that covered 157 years in these places would in theory be tens of thousands of pages long!

The bottom line is that terrorism is a very rare beast in Canada. While the last four decades have been much busier in terms of terrorism activity, they have not been nearly as deadly as in so many other countries. Canada, therefore, is a "mostly" peaceable kingdom.

What should we take from all this? There are several lessons, in my view:

- Terrorism in Canada is so infrequent as to be nearly inconsequential.
- Canadians are at very low risk of being wounded or killed in a terrorist attack.
- The average Canadian does not have to give much thought, if any, to the terrorist threat.
- While this situation could always change at some point there are few signs that it will do so soon.

I say this despite the Air India bombing, the various assassinations, the Islamist extremist plots, and the other sundry extremist attacks in which Canadians were involved. Each one of those left victims and grieving families and this should not be shunted aside. Loss is loss and we need to recognise this and do everything in our power to prevent similar future attacks.

Luckily, Canadians are well served by the organisations sworn to protect them. CSIS, the RCMP, and their partners in Canada and abroad, have stopped attacks from happening here and worked with allies to stop similar action elsewhere. This work will always go largely unthanked and unnoticed, but such is the nature of the profession. As a relatively small intelligence community, it is generally accepted that Canada "punches above its weight."

The bottom line is that without the efforts and dedication of the men and women on the front lines of counterterrorism, Canadians would be worse off. I write this not in a spasm of self-congratulation and mutual back slapping but rather as a statement of the truth.

The next time you read of death and destruction somewhere in the world on an all too frequent basis, take a moment to think of those who toil here in Canada to keep us all safe.

Acknowledgements

I HAVE MADE MANY REFERENCES to the men and women who agreed to speak with me about their experiences in counterterrorism in Canada. This book would have been much poorer without their contributions. I thank each and every one of them for their assistance.

I also wish to acknowledge the professionals I was honoured to work alongside over three decades. Many of the stories and anecdotes included in this book would not have been as meaningful if I had not had the pleasure of sharing our collective responsibilities as part of Canada's security intelligence community.

My family also needs to be recognised. "Dad" was often not at home: evenings, weekends, long foreign trips all interfered with normal family life. That they understood as much as they could about what their father needed to do is much appreciated.

My wife Pat deserves special thanks. Not only has she been at my side for thirty-four years (and counting!), but she also edited several versions of this book and asked me all the right questions (and pointed out places I may want to reword). Thank you!

Appendix
Listed Terrorist Entities in Canada

This list is current up to January 2023.

Abdallah Azzam Brigades (AAB)
Abu Nidal Organisation (ANO)
Abu Sayyaf Group (ASG)
Al-Ashtar Brigades (AAB)
Al-Murabitoun
Al-Muwaqi'un Bil Dima
Al Qaida
Al Qaida in the Arabian Peninsula (AQAP)
Al Qaida in the Indian Subcontinent (AQIS)
Al Qaida in the Islamic Maghreb (AQIM)
Al Shabaab
Al-Aqsa Martyrs' Brigade (AAMB)
Al-Gama'a al-Islamiyya (AGAI)
Ansar Dine
Ansar al-Islam (AI)
Armed Islamic Group (GIA)
Aryan Strikeforce
Asbat Al-Ansar (AAA) (The League of Partisans)
Atomwaffen Division
Aum Shinrikyo
Blood & Honour (B&H)
Babbar Khalsa International (BKI)
Boko Haram
Caucasus Emirate
Combat 18 (C18)

Ejército de Liberación Nacional (ELN)

Euskadi Ta Askatasuna (ETA)

Fatemiyoun Division (FD)

Front du Liberation du Macina

Fuerzas Armadas Revolucionarias de Colombia (FARC)

Gulbuddin Hekmatyar

Gulbuddin Hekmatyar's Faction of the Hezb-e Islami, Hezb-e Islami Gulbuddin (HIG)

Hamas (Harakat Al-Muqawama Al-Islamiya) (Islamic Resistance Movement)

Haqqani Network

Harakat al-Sabireen (HaS)

Harakat ul-Mudjahidin (HuM)

HASAM (Harakat Sawa'd Misr)

Hay'at Tahrir al-Sham

Hizballah

Hizbul Mujahideen

Indian Mujahideen (IM)

International Relief Fund for the Afflicted and Needy - Canada (IRFAN – CANADA)

International Sikh Youth Federation (ISYF)

Islamic Movement of Uzbekistan (IMU)

Islamic Revolutionary Guard Corps' Qods Force

Islamic State

Islamic State - Bangladesh

Islamic State – Democratic Republic of Congo

Islamic State – East Asia

Islamic State in the Greater Sahara

Islamic State – West Africa Province

Islamic State – Khorasan Province (ISKP)

Islamic State – Sinai Province (ISSP)

Islamic State in Libya

Jaish-e-Mohammed (JeM)

Jama'at Nusrat Al-Islam Wal Muslimin (JNIM)

Jaysh Al-Muhajirin Wal-Ansar (JMA)

James Mason

Jemaah Islamiyyah (JI)

Kahane Chai (Kach)
Kurdistan Workers Party (PKK)
Lashkar-e-Jhangvi (LJ)
Lashkar-e-Tayyiba (LeT)
Liberation Tigers of Tamil Eelam (LTTE)
Movement for Oneness and Jihad in West Africa (MOJWA)
Palestine Liberation Front (PLF)
Palestinian Islamic Jihad (PIJ)
Popular Front for the Liberation of Palestine - General Command
   (PFLP-GC)
Popular Front for the Liberation of Palestine (PFLP)
Proud Boys
Russian Imperial Movement
Sendero Luminoso (SL)
Taliban
Tehrik-e-Taliban Pakistan (TTP)
The Base
Three Percenters
World Tamil Movement (WTM)

Endnotes

Introduction

[1] "Global Terrorism Index 2020: Measuring the impact of terrorism on the world," Peace Research, Education and Training Resources, updated December 2020, https://www.visionofhumanity.org/resources/.

[2] Ryan Shaffer, "RAW: a history of India's covert operations," Intelligence and National Security, DOI: 10.1080/02684527.2020.1848299 (https://doi.org/10.1080/02684527.2020.1848299), November 21, 2020, last accessed November 23, 2020.

[3] Gary LaFree, "Terrorism Research: What's Wrong? What's Right? A Conversation with Marc Sageman," Terrorism 360 Episode 12, University of Maryland Study of Terrorism and Responses to Terrorism (START), https://soundcloud.com/user-823068075/t360-episode12-sageman-mixdown, last accessed July 26, 2020.

[4] Stewart Bell, Cold Terror: How Canada Nurtures and Exports Terrorism Around the World (John Wiley & Sons Canada, 2007).

[5] Stewart Bell, The Martyr's Oath: The Apprenticeship of a Homegrown Terrorist (Mississauga: John Wiley & Sons, Canada, 2005).

Chapter 1

[6] Scott Dumonceaux, "The Conspiracy: The Canadian Response to the Order of the Midnight Sun and the Alaska Boundary Dispute," Master's thesis (University of Saskatchewan, September 2013), https://harvest.usask.ca/handle/10388/ETD-2013-09-1234.

[7] Canadian Security Intelligence Service Explanatory Notes (Archived), Solicitor General Canada (undated), https://www.publicsafety.gc.ca/lbrr/

archives/jl%2086.s4%20c32-eng.pdf.

[8] Document provided by contact (former CSIS official).

[9] Document provided by contact (former CSIS official).

[10] "Currently Listed Terrorist Entities," Public Safety Canada, https://www.publicsafety.gc.ca/cnt/ntnl-scrt/cntr-trrrsm/lstd-ntts/index-en.aspx.

[11] Seth Loertscher, Daniel Milton, Bryan Price, and Cynthia Loertscher, The Terrorist Lists: An Examination of the U.S. Government's Counterterrorism Designation Efforts, Combating Terrorism Center, West Point, New York, September 2020, https://ctc.usma.edu/wp-content/uploads/2020/09/The-Terrorist-Lists-report.pdf.

[12] Phil Gurski, "Listing the Proud Boys as a 'terrorist entity' is mostly about politics," Ottawa Citizen, January 13, 2021, https://ottawacitizen.com/opinion/gurski-listing-the-proud-boys-as-a-terrorist-entity-is-mostly-about-politics, last accessed January 17, 2021.

Chapter 2

[13] Phil Gurski, "David Wilson: When Irish terrorists posed a real threat to... Canada!" An Intelligent Look at Terrorism (podcast), Borealis Threat & Risk Consulting, August 11, 2020, https://borealisthreatandrisk.com/podcast-53-david-wilson/.

[14] Arthur H. Rotstein, "Six acquitted in alleged plot to buy detonators for IRA," Associated Press, April 26, 1994, https://apnews.com/529f376176c0c8cc378f7802df49db48, last accessed July 30, 2020.

[15] Andrew Mitrovica, "Canada let IRA members slip through, sources say," Globe and Mail, October 13, 2001, https://www.theglobeandmail.com/news/national/canada-let-ira-members-slip-through-sources-say/article4154732/.

[16] D'Arcy Jenish, "For the Bloc Quebecois, the October Crisis is a political weapon," Globe and Mail October 2, 2020, https://www.theglobeandmail.com/opinion/article-for-the-bloc-quebecois-the-october-crisis-is-a-modern-day-political/, last accessed October 22, 2020.

[17] Dan Bilefsky, "A polarizing documentary spurs debate over a violent time in Quebec," New York Times, December 6, 2020, https://www.nytimes.com/2020/12/06/world/canada/quebec-rose-october-crisis.html.

[18] Patrick Martin, "Ottawa tribute to slain Turkish envoy opens old wounds," Globe and Mail, September 19, 2012, https://www.theglobeandmail.com/

news/world/ottawa-tribute-to-slain-turkish-envoy-reopens-old-wounds/ article4555832/, last accessed September 7, 2020.

[19] Reuters, "3 Armenians Convicted in Attack in Ottawa," The New York Times, November 1, 1986, www.nytimes.com/1986/11/01/world/ around-the-world-3-armenians-convicted-in-attack-in-ottawa.html, last accessed September 7, 2020.

[20] Charles Forrester, "Armenia-Azerbaijan territorial dispute remains critical flashpoint," Jane's Defence News, September 14, 2020, https://www.janes. com/defence-news/news-detail/armenia-azerbaijan-territorial-dispute- remains-critical-flashpoint.

[21] "Anti-Cuba Terrorist Attacks – The Canadian Connection," Canadian Network on Cuba, July 2012, https://canadiannetworkoncuba.ca/ tribunal/Media/The%20Canadian%20Connection.pdf.

[22] Tom Blackwell, "Fight for a foreign homeland waged in Canada," National Post, August 27, 2020.

[23] As cited by Terry Milewski in "Khalistan: A Project of Pakistan," Macdonald Laurier Institute, September 2020, page 15, https:// macdonaldlaurier.ca/files/pdf/20200820_Khalistan_Air_India_ Milewski_PAPER_FWeb.pdf?mc_cid=3acb7f8abd&mc_ eid=682afa06f8, last accessed September 9, 2020.

[24] Stewart Bell "'Match. Denied': Secret documents show why CSIS put 2 Canadians on no-fly list," Global News July 8, 2020, https://globalnews. ca/news/7147226/secret-documents-csis-canadians-on-no-fly-list/, last accessed September 9, 2020.

[25] The Tribune, "Punjab police bust pro-Khalistan terror module: 2 arrested," September 15, 2020 https://www.tribuneindia.com/news/punjab/ punjab-police-bust-pro-khalistan-terror-module-2-arrested-141537, last accessed September 15, 2020.

[26] Tom Blackwell, "Canadian Sikh group alleges censorship after Indian government asks Twitter to delete its post," National Post, September 16, 2020, https://nationalpost.com/news/canada/canadian-sikh-group- alleges-censorship-after-indian-government-asks-twitter-to-delete-its- post/wcm/80d0aad0-30e6-4e84-84a6-2ba0a51a34e7/, last accessed September 16, 2020.

[27] Robert D. McFadden, "Iran Rebels Hit Missions in 10 Nations," New York Times, April 6, 1992, https://www.nytimes.com/1992/04/06/ world/iran-rebels-hit-missions-in-10-nations.html.

[28] CBC News, "Key Iranian dissident released in France," July 3, 2003, https://www.cbc.ca/news/canada/key-iranian-dissident-released-in-france-1.405349, last accessed September 7, 2020.

[29] The Canadian Press, "Canada drops Iranian group MEK from terror list," CBC News, December 20, 2012, https://www.cbc.ca/news/politics/canada-drops-iranian-group-mek-from-terror-list-1.1239066, last accessed September 7, 2020.

[30] Stewart Bell, "Echoes of Iran," National Post, October 15, 2011, https://nationalpost.com/news/echoes-of-iran, last accessed September 10, 2020.

Chapter 3

[31] Chris Cobb, "Paris synagogue bombing shattered lives," Ottawa Citizen, November 6, 2010, http://www.ottawacitizen.com/life/Paris+synagogue+bombing+shattered+lives/3788723/story.html, last accessed December 3, 2020.

[32] David Cochrane, "Hassan Diab urges federal government to settle $90 million claim alleging 'wrongful extradition,'" CBC News, February 7, 2020, https://www.cbc.ca/news/politics/hassan-diab-extradition-terror-france-1.5455930, last accessed October 7, 2020.

[33] John Goddard, "Forgotten Islamist terror plot targeted Toronto," Toronto Star, August 31, 2010, https://www.thestar.com/news/canada/2010/08/31/forgotten_islamist_terror_plot_targeted_toronto.html, last accessed September 29, 2020.

[34] Phil Gurski, "Today in terrorism: October 3, 1991," Today in Terrorism (blog), Borealis Threat & Risk Consulting, October 3, 2019, https://borealisthreatandrisk.com/today-in-terrorism-october-3-1991/.

[35] Stewart Bell, Cold Terror: How Canada nurtures and exports terrorism around the world, (John Wiley and Sons Canada, 2004), 179.

[36] Eric Grenier, "Majority of Canadians oppose Omar Khadr settlement, poll suggests," CBC News, July 10, 2017, https://www.cbc.ca/news/politics/grenier-khadr-poll-1.4198306, last accessed September 29, 2020.

[37] "Interview Maha Elsamna & Zaynab Khadr," Frontline, PBS, https://www.pbs.org/wgbh/pages/frontline/shows/khadr/interviews/mahazaynab.html, last accessed September 29, 2020.

[38] CBC News, "Khadr lawyer frightened off by death threat," December 4, 2003, https://www.cbc.ca/news/canada/khadr-lawyer-frightened-off-by-

death-threat-1.381923, last accessed November 26, 2020.

[39] Kathleen Harris, "Judge dismisses all 19 charges against ex-Afghanistan hostage Joshua Boyle in sexual assault case," CBC News, December 18, 2019, https://www.cbc.ca/news/politics/joshua-boyle-caitlan-coleman-verdict-1.5400633, last accessed November 26, 2020.

[40] Ward Elcock, "Section III: The Terrorism Threat to Canada." Submission to the Special Committee of the Senate on Security and Intelligence, June 24, 1998.

[41] Phil Gurski, "Podcast 31 – Interview with former security intelligence and counter terrorism operative Mubin Shaikh," An Intelligent Look at Terrorism (podcast), Borealis Threat & Risk Consulting, February 2020, https://borealisthreatandrisk.com/episode-31-interview-with-former-security-intelligence-and-counter-terrorism-operative-mubin-shaikh/.

[42] Adrian Humphries "Reformed Toronto 18 terror plotter given green light to become a licensed lawyer" National Post March 22, 2022 https://www.nationalpost.com/news/   canada/reformed-toronto-18-terror-plotter-given-green-light-to-become-a-licensed-lawyer

[43] Michele Mandel "Toronto 18 bomb plotter denied parole but can visit GTA anytime" Toronto Sun September 15, 2022 https://torontosun.com/news/local-news/mandel-toronto-18-bomb-plotter-denied-full-parole-but-can-visit-gta-anytime

[44] Stewart Bell "Toronto 18 bomb plot leader denied parole despite claiming to be non-violent" May 28, 2021 https://globalnews.ca/news/7902466/toronto-18-leader-denied-parole-non-violent/

[45] The Canadian Press, "Via Rail terror case: Jury error does not warrant new trial, Crown argues," Global News, October 7, 2020, https://globalnews.ca/news/7382903/via-rail-terror-case-error-jury-not-warrant-new-trial/, last accessed October 8, 2020.

[46] The Canadian Press, "No new trial for 2 men convicted in Via Rail terror case: Supreme Court," CBC News, October 8, 2020, https://www.cbc.ca/news/politics/supreme-court-no-new-trial-1.5754384, last accessed October 8, 2020.

[47] Jason Proctor, "RCMP entrapment of B.C. couple in Legislature plot was a 'travesty of justice,'" CBC News, December 19, 2018, https://www.cbc.ca/news/canada/british-columbia/john-nuttall-amanda-korody-2018-1.4952431, last accessed October 9, 2020.

[48] Rafferty Baker "Couple accused in 2013 plot to plant bombs at B.C.

Legislature sue police" CBC News August 30, 2022 https://www.cbc.ca/news/canada/british-columbia/nuttall-korody-lawsuit-filed-1.6567388

[49] The Canadian Press, "Man accused in military centre stabbing acquitted of terror charges, not criminally responsible," May 14, 2018, https://www.cbc.ca/news/canada/toronto/toronto-ayanle-hassan-ali-verdict-1.4661721, last accessed October 12, 2020.

[50] CBC News, "Man who attacked soldiers in 2016 shouldn't have been acquitted of terror charges: Crown," June 24, 2019, https://www.cbc.ca/news/canada/toronto/ayanle-hassan-ali-crown-appeal-1.5187613, last accessed October 12, 2020.

[51] Michael Friscolanti, "How to stop a terrorist," Macleans, August 29, 2016, page 22, found online at https://archive.macleans.ca/article/2016/8/29/how-to-stop-a-terrorist.

[52] Alyshah Hasham, "In highly unusual trial, Rehab Dughmosh admits to attacking Scarborough Canadian Tire 'for ISIS' - but refuses to enter plea," Hamilton Spectator, January 17, 2019, https://www.thespec.com/news/ontario/2019/01/17/in-highly-unusual-trial-rehab-dughmosh-admits-to-attacking-scarborough-canadian-tire-for-isis-but-refuses-to-enter-plea.html, last accessed October 12, 2020.

[53] CBC News, "Woman guilty of terror charges for Canadian Tire attack sentenced to 7 years in prison," February 14, 2019, https://www.cbc.ca/news/canada/toronto/rehab-dughmosh-canadian-tire-sentencing-1.5018987, last accessed November 26, 2020.

[54] Jonny Wakefield, "Everything we know about the man charged in Edmonton's truck attack from the woman who knows him best," Edmonton Journal, September 28, 2018, https://edmontonjournal.com/news/crime/who-is-abdulahi-hasan-sharif-one-year-later-everything-we-know-about-the-alleged-edmonton-attacker, last accessed October 12, 2020.

[55] Colette Derorwiz, "Abdulahi Sharif sentenced to 28 years for trying to kill Edmonton police officer, pedestrians," Global News, December 13, 2019, https://globalnews.ca/news/6295290/sharif-sentenced-edmonton-vehicle-uhaul-police-officer-attack/, last accessed October 12, 2020.

[56] Catharine Tunney, "Kingston teen pleads guilty to four terrorism charges in relation to alleged bomb plot," CBC News, July 28, 2020, https://www.cbc.ca/news/politics/kingston-teen-guilty-plea-1.5665891, last accessed November 19, 2020.

[57] Al Jazeera, "Two sentenced over Bulgaria bus bombing blamed

on Hizballah," September 21, 2020, https://www.aljazeera.com/news/2020/9/21/two-sentenced-over-bulgaria-bus-bombing-blamed-on-hezbollah, last accessed October 13, 2020.

58 CBC News, "Suicide bomber killed in Iraq part of wider jihadi base in Calgary," June 3, 2014, https://www.cbc.ca/news/canada/suicide-bomber-killed-in-iraq-part-of-wider-jihadi-base-in-calgary-1.2663890, last accessed October 13, 2020.

59 Stewart Bell, "Canadian linked to terrorist group was killed in a suicide attack in Somalia: community source," National Post, April 15, 2013, https://nationalpost.com/news/canadian-linked-to-terrorist-group-was-killed-in-suicide-attack-in-somalia-community-source, last accessed October 13, 2020.

60 Michelle Shephard, "Meet the Canadian woman who runs a safe house for Al Qaeda suicide bombers," Toronto Star, July 12, 2012, https://www.thestar.com/news/world/2012/07/12/meet_the_canadian_woman_who_runs_a_safe_house_for_al_qaeda_suicide_bombers.html, last accessed December 1, 2020.

61 The Economic Times, "Dhaka attack: hostages were killed within twenty minutes of assault," July 4, 2016, https://economictimes.indiatimes.com/news/international/world-news/dhaka-attack-hostages-were-killed-within-20-minutes-after-assault/articleshow/53044296.cms, last accessed October 12, 2020.

62 Associated Press, "Bangladesh police kill Canadian suspect in restaurant attack," CBC News, August 27, 2016, https://www.cbc.ca/news/world/bangladesh-restaurant-attack-1.3738298, last accessed October 12, 2020.

63 Stewart Bell, "Interpol poster shows dramatic transformation of B.C. man charged with joining terrorist group in Syria," National Post, September 4, 2014, https://nationalpost.com/news/canada/interpol-poster-shows-dramatic-transformation-of-b-c-man-charged-with-joining-terrorist-group-in-syria, last accessed November 8, 2020.

64 Tristin Hopper, "Man charged under new terror law 'a polite kid' who dreamed of joining RCMP: family, associates say," National Post, July 24, 2014, https://nationalpost.com/news/canada/man-charged-under-new-terror-law-a-polite-kid-who-dreamed-of-joining-rcmp-family-associates-say, last accessed November 8, 2020.

65 Devin Heroux, Nazim Baksh, "Calgary mosque tainted by 'dark element' of radicalization to close doors this week," CBC News, March 30, 2017,

https://www.cbc.ca/news/canada/calgary/calgary-mosque-radicalization-8th-and-8th-1.4042692, last accessed January 17, 2020.

[66] Phil Gurski, "Podcast 45 – Christianne Boudreau: My child died fighting for a terrorist group," An Intelligent Look at Terrorism (podcast), June 9, 2020, https://borealisthreatandrisk.com/podcast-45-christianne-boudreau/.

[67] Nadim Roberts, "Gregory and Collin Gordon, Calgary brothers, join ranks of Canadians fighting for ISIS," CBC News, August 29, 2014, https://www.cbc.ca/news/gregory-and-collin-gordon-calgary-brothers-join-ranks-of-canadians-fighting-for-isis-1.2749673, last accessed November 12, 2020.

[68] Stewart Bell and Andrew Miller, "Canadian jihadi Farah Mohamed Shirdon killed in Iraq airstrike in 2015: U.S. military," Global News, September 7, 2017, https://globalnews.ca/news/3722685/canadian-jihadi-farah-mohamed-shirdon-killed-in-iraq-airstrike-in-2015-u-s-military/, last accessed November 12, 2020.

[69] Dawn Walton, "I wanted to join the insurgency but nothing ever happened," Globe and Mail, February 9, 2013, https://www.theglobeandmail.com/news/national/i-wanted-to-join-the-insurgency-but-nothing-ever-happened/article8421438/?page=3, last accessed November 12, 2020.

[70] Dawn Walton, "I wanted to join the insurgency but nothing ever happened," Globe and Mail, February 9, 2013, https://www.theglobeandmail.com/news/national/i-wanted-to-join-the-insurgency-but-nothing-ever-happened/article8421438/?page=3, last accessed November 12, 2020.

[71] Bill Graveland, "Calgary man accused of joining Islamic State faces terrorism charges," National Post, July 22, 2020, https://nationalpost.com/news/calgary-man-faces-terrorism-charges-after-allegedly-joining-islamic-state/wcm/a8fc3a4d-2a47-4298-abe1-90779a08820e/, last accessed November 18, 2020.

[72] Stewart Bell, "Muhanad Mahmoud al-Farekh former University of Manitoba student charged with supporting terrorism," National Post, April 2, 2015, http://news.nationalpost.com/news/canada/muhanad-mahmoud-al-farekh-former-university-of-manitoba-student-charged-with-supporting-terrorism, last accessed December 7, 2020.

[73] CBC News, "Windsor's Mohamed El Shaer arrested on terrorism peace bond," June 17, 2016, https://www.cbc.ca/news/canada/windsor/mohamed-el-shaer-terrorism-1.3640678, last accessed November 18, 2020.

[74] Stewart Bell, The Martyr's Oath: The Apprenticeship of a Homegrown Terrorist (Mississauga: John Wiley & Sons, Canada, 2005).

[75] CBC News, "Ontario man convicted of terrorism offences re-arrested, could pose public safety risk: RCMP," August 24, 2020, https://www.cbc.ca/news/canada/toronto/kevin-omar-mohamed-arrested-again-terror-ontario-1.5698191, last accessed November 18, 2020.

[76] National Post, "Who is Awso Peshdary? The case against an alleged Ottawa extremist who police allege recruited for ISIL," February 27, 2016, https://nationalpost.com/news/canada/who-is-awso-peshdary-the-case-against-an-alleged-ottawa-extremist-who-police-say-radicalized-at-risk-youth, last accessed November 18, 2020.

[77] Gary Dimmock, "CSIS used intel gathered illegally, withheld evidence favourable to accused Ottawa ISIS recruiter," Ottawa Citizen, August 27, 2020, https://ottawacitizen.com/news/local-news/csis-used-intel-gathered-illegally-withheld-evidence-favourable-to-accused-ottawa-isis-recruiter, last accessed November 18, 2020.

[78] Gary Dimmock, "Ottawa terrorist accused of trying to radicalize inmates released from prison, living in Calgary halfway house," Ottawa Citizen, February 7, 2020, https://ottawacitizen.com/news/local-news/0207-carlos, last accessed November 19, 2020.

[79] Stewart Bell, "Man convicted of trying to join ISIS granted overnight privileges to visit ski resort with girlfriend," Global News, November 11, 2020, https://globalnews.ca/news/7455403/man-convicted-isis-overnight-privileges-ski-resort/, last accessed November 19, 2020.

[80] John Paul Tasker, "Toronto-area woman arrested on terrorism charges after travel to Turkey," CBC News, August 26, 2020, https://www.cbc.ca/news/politics/toronto-woman-arrested-terrorism-charges-1.5701147, last accessed November 19, 2020.

[81] Bobby Hristova, "Burlington, Ont. man faces terrorism hoax charge after claiming to be ISIS member," CBC News, September 25, 2020, https://www.cbc.ca/news/canada/hamilton/shehroze-chaudhry-terrorism-hoax-charge-1.5739814, last accessed November 19, 2020.

[82] CBC News, "Montreal couple cleared of terrorism charges, boyfriend guilty of explosives-related offence," December 19, 2017, https://www.cbc.ca/news/canada/Montreal/Montreal-couple-cleared-of-terror-charges-boyfriend-guilty-of-explosives-related-offence-1.4452720, last accessed November 19, 2020.

[83] The National (UAE), "Swedish female ISIS supporters may be tried in Syria for terrorism offences," October 12, 2020, https://www.thenational.ae/world/swedish-female-isis-supporters-may-be-tried-in-syria-for-terrorism-offences-1.1092495?utm_source=iterable&utm_medium=email&utm_campaign=1607733, last accessed October 13, 2020.

[84] Richard Fadden, Proceedings of the Special Senate Committee on, April 23, 2012, https://sencanada.ca/en/Content/Sen/committee/411/antr/02ev-49469-e.

[85] Duncan Gardham, "7/7 inquest: Mohammed Sidique Khan on MI5's radar before 9/11," The Telegraph, May 6, 2011, http://www.telegraph.co.uk/news/uknews/terrorism-in-the-uk/8497204/77-inquest-Mohammed-Sidique-Khan-on-MI5s-radar-before-911.html, last accessed December 7, 2020.

Chapter 4

[86] Jonathan Montpetit, "Quebec mosque shooter's sentence reduced as appeals court rules consecutive life sentences are unconstitutional," CBC News, November 26, 2020, https://www.cbc.ca/news/canada/Montreal/court-of-appeal-decision-bissonnette-1.5816508, last accessed November 26, 2020.

[87] Marie-Helene Hetu, "How Alexandre Bissonnette - and other mass shooters – could be stopped before they kill," CBC News, October 19, 2019, https://www.cbc.ca/news/canada/alexandre-bissonnette-mass-shooters-1.5326201, last accessed November 26, 2020.

[88] Shanfa Nasser, "Terror charges in alleged 'incel' – inspired stabbing could force reckoning of Canada's terrorism laws: experts," CBC News, May 20, 2020, https://www.cbc.ca/news/canada/toronto/incel-canada-terrorism-1.5577015, last accessed September 22, 2020.

[89] Shanifa Nasser 'Toronto spa killer pleads guilty to murder in deadly sword attack, cites van attacker as 'inspiration' CBC News September 14, 2022 https://www.cbc.ca/news/canada/toronto/incel-massage-parlour-guilty-1.6582534

[90] Stewart Bell and Catherine McDonald 'London attack suspect charged with terrorism' Global News June 14, 2021 http://globalnews.

ca/news/7942926/london-attack-suspect-terrorism/

[91] Phil Gurski, "Podcast 43 – Naama Kates and 'The Incel Project,'" An Intelligent Look at Terrorism, May 26, 2020, https://borealisthreatandrisk.com/podcast-43-naama-kates-the-incel-project/.

[92] Brian Platt, "For the first time, Canada adds white supremacist neo-Nazi groups to its list of terrorist organizations," National Post, June 26, 2019, https://nationalpost.com/news/politics/for-the-first-time-canada-adds-white-supremacist-neo-nazi-groups-to-its-list-of-terrorist-organizations, last accessed September 22, 2020.

[93] John Paul Tasker 'Canada names the Proud Boys, neo-Nazis as terrorists' CBC News February 3, 2021 http://www.cbc.ca/news/politics/canada-proud-boys-terrorists-1.5899186

[94] Tristan Wheeler 'Ottawa councillor says Freedom Convoy protesters are 'terrorists who are torturing locals' Narcity February 6, 2022 https://www.narcity.com/ottawa-councillor-says-freedom-convoy-protestors-are-terrorists-who-are-torturing-locals

[95] David Pugliese, "Analysis: New defence chief could face pressure to act against racists and extremists in the ranks," Ottawa Citizen, September 12, 2020, https://ottawacitizen.com/news/national/defence-watch/analysis-new-defence-chief-could-face-pressure-to-act-against-racists-and-extremists-in-the-ranks/wcm/4990657e-62ea-4dea-8942-095385bccbbb/, last accessed September 22, 2020.

[96] Amazon (website), Books, https://www.amazon.ca/Bayou-Pigs-Stewart-Bell/dp/1443427640.

[97] Phil Gurski, "How serious is the far-right extremist threat in Canada? Are we taking it seriously enough?" An Intelligent Look a Terrorism, October 6, 2020, https://borealisthreatandrisk.com/podcast-62-barbara-perry/.

[98] Paul Karp, "Asio reveals up to 40% of its counter-terrorism cases involve far-right violent extremism," The Guardian, September 22, 2020, https://www.theguardian.com/australia-news/2020/sep/22/asio-reveals-up-to-40-of-its-counter-terrorism-cases-involve-far-right-violent-extremism?utm_source=iterable&utm_medium=email&utm_campaign=1549072_/, last accessed September 23, 2020.

[99] Internet Movie Database (IMDB) (website), https://www.imdb.com/title/tt0146287/plotsummary?ref_=tt_stry_pl.

[100] Squamish Real Estate Group (website), "The Squamish Five: Urban Guerillas in the Midst," https://squamish.com/the-squamish-five-urban-guerillas-in-the-midst/.

Chapter 5

[101] Ian Holliday 'So far, no link to existing protests found in Coastal GasLink attack investigation, RCMP say' CTV News February 20, 2022 https://bc.ctvnews.ca/so-far-no-link-to-existing-protests-found-in-coastal-gaslink-attack-investigation-rcmp-say-1.5789194

[102] Amy Judd 'Wet'suwet'en Nation condemns northern B.C. pipeline attack as new images released' Global News February 18, 2022 https://globalnews.ca/news/8631596/northern-bc-pipeline-attack-images-security-video/

[103] Nicole Chavez 'At least 4 Catholic churches were destroyed on indigenous land in a week' CNN June 29, 2021 https://www.cnn.com/2021/06/29/americas/canada-church-fires-indigenous-land/index.html

[104] Patrick Wintour, "Five eyes alliance could expand in scope to counteract China," The Guardian, July 20, 2020, https://www.theguardian.com/uk-news/2020/jul/29/five-eyes-alliance-could-expand-in-scope-to-counteract-china, last accessed September 28, 2020.

[105] BBC, "The 'ticking bomb' problem," http://www.bbc.co.uk/ethics/torture/ethics/tickingbomb_1.shtml, accessed July 26, 2020.

[106] Jim Bronskill, "CSIS mole defends work with white supremacists," Globe and Mail, August 11, 2004, https://www.theglobeandmail.com/news/national/csis-mole-defends-work-with-white-supremacists/article18269738/, accessed January 17, 2021.

[107] Andrew Duffy, "Ottawa terror suspect Mohamed Harkat denied state-funded lawyer in extradition fight," Post Media, July 6, 2020, https://www.thechronicleherald.ca/news/canada/ottawa-terror-suspect-denied-state-funded-lawyer-in-extradition-fight-470199/, accessed January 17, 2021.

[108] Perspectives | How woke and cancel culture undermine CT understanding (borealisthreatandrisk.com)

[109] Grant Robertson, "What happened with Canada's pandemic alert system? The GPHIN controversy explained," Globe and Mail, October 13, 2020, https://www.theglobeandmail.com/canada/article-what-happened-with-canadas-pandemic-alert-system-the-gphin/, accessed January 17, 2021.

DOUBLE†DAGGER
— www.doubledagger.ca —

Double Dagger Books is Canada's only military-focused publisher. Conflict and warfare have shaped human history since before we began to record it. The earliest stories that we know of, passed on as oral tradition, speak of war, and more importantly, the essential elements of the human condition that are revealed under its pressure. We are dedicated to publishing material that, while rooted in conflict, transcends the idea of "war" as merely a genre. Fiction, non- fiction, and stuff that defies categorization, we want to read it all.

Because if you want peace, study war.

Phil Gurski is the President and CEO of Borealis Threat and Risk Consulting Ltd. (www.borealisthreatandrisk.com) and a Distinguished Fellow in National Security at the University of Ottawa's Professional Development Institute (PDI). He worked as a senior strategic analyst at CSIS (Canadian Security Intelligence Service) from 2001-2015, specializing in violent Islamist-inspired homegrown terrorism and radicalisation. From 1983 to 2001 he was employed as a senior multilingual analyst at Communications Security Establishment (CSE – Canada's signals intelligence agency), specialising in the Middle East. He also served as senior special advisor in the National Security Directorate at Public Safety Canada from 2013, focusing on community outreach and training on radicalisation to violence, until his retirement from the federal civil service in May 2015, and as consultant for the Ontario Provincial Police's Anti-Terrorism Section (PATS) from May to October 2015. He was the Director of Security and Intelligence at the SecDev Group from June 2018 to July 2019, focusing on Islamist terrorism online. From October 2019 to April 2022 he was the Director of the National Security Program at the University of Ottawa's PDI.

www.ingramcontent.com/pod-product-compliance
Lightning Source LLC
Chambersburg PA
CBHW071325120626
46546CB00002B/439